Table of Conten

Introduction

The new Cuisinart Air Fryer Toaster Oven is an advanced multi-functional cooking appliance that works on hot air circulation technology. It can fry, bake, convection bake, toast, warm, broil, convection broil with little to no oil. With seven functions, it can do everything from toast bread and reheat leftovers to roast a whole chicken. The capacity is large enough to fit six slices of toast or a 12-inch pizza. The unit comes with a baking pan, an air fryer basket, and a recipe book. Air frying requires no preheating, so it's ready to cook as soon as you load the food in.

It is a versatile appliance and it features a powerful 1800-watt heating element that ensures even cooking, while the four-quart capacity allows you to cook large meals. The digital control panel makes it easy to select the desired cooking function, and the unit comes with an air fryer basket, baking pan, and oven rack. It is an all-in-one appliance that will make a great addition to your kitchen.

The Cuisinart Air Fryer Oven Cookbook is the perfect guide for anyone who wants to learn how to use their air fryer oven to make delicious, healthy meals. Featuring over 100 recipes specifically designed for air fryer ovens, this cookbook covers everything from breakfast dishes to desserts. If you want to make a quick and easy weeknight meal or want to simply impress your friends and family with a gourmet dish, the Cuisinart Air Fryer Oven Cookbook has you covered. In addition to step-by-step instructions, each recipe includes tips on how to get the best results, as well as mouthwatering photos of the finished dish.

Fundamentals of Cuisinart Air Fryer Oven

Whereas the Cuisinart air fryer toaster oven is a new and versatile appliance that is used for a variety of cooking tasks. Air frying uses less oil than traditional frying methods, so it's a healthier option.

It has a wide range of temperatures, so you can easily cook your food to perfection. The appliance also has a built-in self-clean function, so you don't have to worry about messy clean-up. And if you're looking for a toaster oven that can do it all, the Cuisinart air fryer toaster oven is the perfect choice.

What is Cuisinart Air Fryer Oven?

▲ Cuisinart Air Fryer Oven is a kitchen appliance that combines the functions of an air fryer, toaster oven, and convection oven. It is manufactured by the American home appliance brand Cuisinart.

▲ The product was first introduced in 2018 and quickly gained popularity due to its compact size, multiple functions, and ability to cook food quickly and evenly.

▲ The Air Fryer Toaster Oven uses hot air to fry food, eliminating the need for oil or butter. It also has a built-in toaster oven function that can be used to toast bread, bagels, and other pastries.

▲ In addition, the Cuisinart Air Fryer Toaster Oven has a convection feature that circulates hot air throughout the oven, cooking food more evenly and quickly.

Benefits of Using It

Who doesn't love fried foods? The crispy, salty goodness is hard to resist. But fried foods are also notoriously unhealthy, loaded with fat and calories. That's where the Cuisinart Air Fryer Toaster Oven comes in. This innovative appliance uses cutting-edge technology to fry foods with little or no oil, making it a healthier alternative to traditional frying methods. No wonder the Cuisinart Air Fryer Toaster Oven is becoming so popular. It's the perfect way to enjoy delicious fried foods without all the guilt.

When it comes to kitchen appliances, the Cuisinart air fryer oven is one of the best. This handy appliance can not only toast and air fry your food, but it also has a host of other functions that make it a must-have for any kitchen. Here are 15 benefits of owning a Cuisinart air fryer toaster oven:

It's multifunctional
The Cuisinart air fryer toaster oven can do more than just toast and air fry your food. It can also bake, broil and warm your meals. This makes it perfect for those who want to save time in the kitchen.

Cooks food evenly
The Cuisinart Air Fryer Toaster Oven uses convection cooking for the purpose of circulating hot air around food, cooking it evenly on all sides. This prevents hot spots that can cause uneven cooking and burned food.

Retains nutrients
Because the Cuisinart Air Fryer Toaster Oven cooks food quickly and evenly, it helps to retain more of the nutrients than other cooking methods. This is especially beneficial for foods that are high in vitamins and minerals.

Reduces fat and calories
The Cuisinart Air Fryer Toaster Oven uses little or no oil to cook food. This reduces the fat and calorie content of meals, making them healthier overall.

Can accommodate large quantities
This Cuisinart Air Fryer Toaster Oven is large enough to accommodate large quantities of food. This is ideal for cooking for a crowd or meal prepping for the week ahead.

Lightweight
The Cuisinart air fryer toaster oven weighs just over 10 pounds, making it easy to move around as needed.

It comes with a removable drip and crumb tray
The drip tray makes it easy to deal with the food and you don't have to worry about oil splatters when you're cooking with this appliance. Whereas the crumb tray makes cleanup quick and easy after each use. Simply remove the tray and empty it into the trash or compost bin.

It comes with an instruction booklet
This booklet provides step-by-step instructions on how to use the different functions of the Cuisinart Air Fryer Toaster Oven, as well as helpful tips on how to get the best results when cooking with an air fryer.

One-year warranty
While buying the Cuisinart Air Fryer Toaster Oven you get a one-year warranty that ensures that you will get help from customer service if you experience any problems with your appliance within the first year of ownership, taking away any worry about making a long-term investment.

Easy to clean
It has a nonstick interior that makes cleanup quick and easy. There is also no need to worry about oil splatters with this appliance.

Economical
This Oven is an economical appliance to use because it doesn't require oil or butter for cooking. This saves money on groceries and promotes healthy eating habits.

Durable
The Cuisinart Air Fryer Toaster Oven is made from high-quality materials that make it highly durable and long lasting. This ensures that you get years of use from this appliance without having to replace it frequently.

Attractive design
The Cuisinart Air Fryer Oven has a sleek and modern design that looks great in any kitchen décor scheme.

Safe
The Cuisinart Air Fryer Toaster Oven has an automatic shut-off feature that prevents it from overheating. This makes it a safe appliance to use in the kitchen.

Reasonable Price
Considering all the Cuisinart Air Fryer Toaster Oven offers, the price is quite affordable, making it a great value for your money.

ETL certified

The Cuisinart Air Fryer Toaster Oven meets high safety standards, giving you peace of mind when using it in your home.

Energy efficient

The Cuisinart Air Fryer Toaster Oven is energy-efficient. It uses 70% less energy than a conventional oven, so you can save money on your energy bills.

Excellent customer service

If you have any problems with your Cuisinart Air Fryer Toaster Oven, simply contact customer service for assistance. The company's friendly and helpful representatives will be more than happy to help you troubleshoot any issues you may be having or answer any questions you may have about the product.

Features of Cuisinart Air Fryer Oven

Some features of The Cuisinart Air Fryer Oven that make it a unique and useful appliance are

Power Indicator

▲ The Cuisinart Air Fryer Oven is a unique and innovative kitchen appliance. Not only does it have the ability to air fry your food, but it also has a built-in toaster oven.

▲ This allows you to cook multiple items at once, making it a perfect appliance for those who love to entertain. One of the best features of the Cuisinart Air Fryer Toaster Oven is the Power On Light Indicator. This light will turn on and remain lit when the oven is in use. This is a great safety feature that allows you to see if the oven is still on, even if you're not in the kitchen. It's also a helpful way to know when your food is done cooking.

▲ The Power On Light Indicator is just one of the many reasons why the Cuisinart Air Fryer Toaster Oven is an amazing kitchen appliance.

Timer Dial

▲ This dial can be used to set the desired cooking time for all functions except the Toast function.

▲ Once the desired time has been set, the unit will power on and begin the cooking cycle. When the time is complete, the unit will power off. This feature is particularly useful for ensuring that food is cooked evenly and thoroughly.

▲ In addition, it allows users to free up their hands for other tasks while the appliance is in use.

Temperature Dial

▲ The Cuisinart Air Fryer Toaster Oven comprises of an Oven Temperature Dial that allows you to set the desired temperature for your food. This is an important feature as it helps to ensure that your food is cooked evenly and at the right temperature.

▲ The dial also has an indicator light that lets you know when the oven is preheated and ready to use.

Function Dial

▲ The Function Dial is used to select the desired cooking method, and the corresponding settings will be automatically applied. For example, if you select the Toast setting, the oven will preheat to the ideal temperature for toasting bread.

▲ The Air-Fry setting is perfect for creating crispy foods without using oil, and the Convection Bake setting can be used for baking cakes and cookies. Whether you want to warm up leftovers or bake a dessert, the Cuisinart Air Fryer Toaster Oven can help you get the job done.

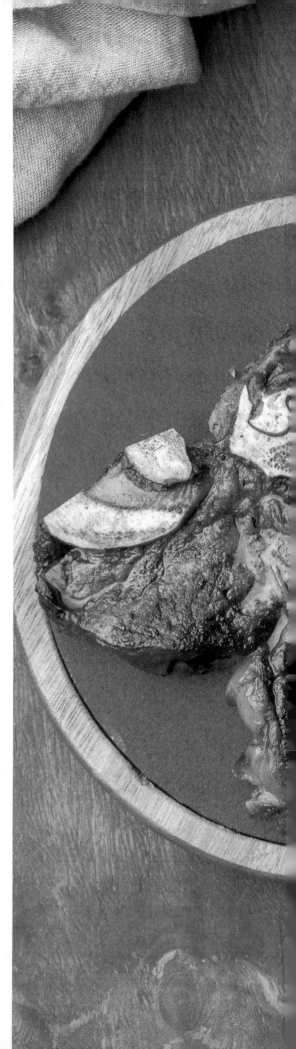

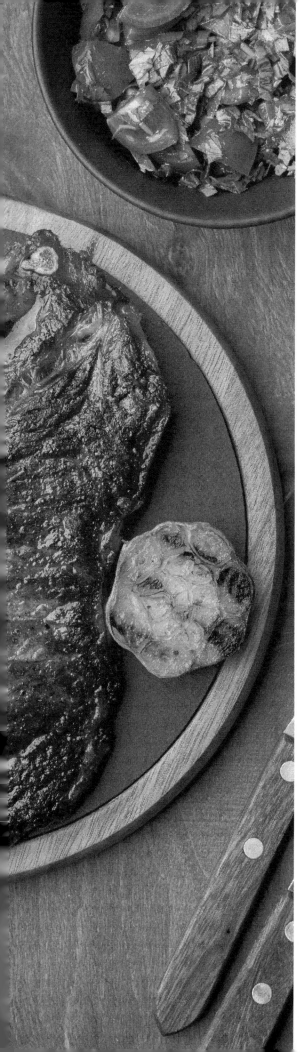

Light Button

▲ The Cuisinart Air Fryer Oven has a light button that turns on the interior oven light. This is a highly convenient feature that allows you to see the food as it cooks.

▲ The light will turn off automatically when the oven is not in use. Please note that it comprises of a bulb-saver feature allowing the light to work only when the oven is being used.

▲ The light will not work whenever power is off. This is a safety feature that prevents the bulb from overheating.

Easy to Clean

▲ The Cuisinart Air Fryer Toaster Oven is equipped with an easy to clean interior. The sides of the oven are completely coated, providing an easy-to-clean surface.

▲ The interior is also nonstick, so food release and cleanup are quick and easy.

▲ The Air Fryer Toaster Oven also features a removable crumb tray that can be washed in the dishwasher.

▲ For more stubborn messes, the interior can be wiped clean with a damp cloth. With its easy clean interior, the Cuisinart Air Fryer Toaster Oven is a hassle-free addition to any kitchen.

Safety Auto Off Door Switch

This oven has a safety auto Off switch that cuts off power when the oven door is opened. This feature helps to prevent accidents and ensures that the appliance is used safely.

Air Fryer Basket

With the Air Fryer Basket, you can maximize your cooking results by using it in conjunction with the Air Fry function. The basket is designed to nest within the baking pan, so it's always ready to work when you need it. And since it's made of non-stick material, cleanup is a breeze.

Oven Rack

▲ The Air Fryer Toaster Oven has a removable oven rack that can be used in two positions. Position 1 (bottom) is for conventional baking and browning, while Position 2 (top) is 50% stopped, so the rack only comes halfway out of the oven, ideal for dehydrating or keeping food warm.

▲ The rack can be removed from Position 2 by first lifting the front of the rack and then sliding it out.

▲ When not in use, the oven rack should be stored in a safe, dry place. For best results, follow the instructions in the manual when using the Cuisinart Air Fryer Toaster Oven.

Baking Pan

▲ The Toaster Oven comes with a Baking Pan/Drip Tray for your convenience. This pan can be used alone when baking or roasting.

▲ When using the Air Fryer Basket, the Baking Pan can also be used for Air Frying. This is a great feature that allows you to have more options when cooking with your Air Fryer Toaster Oven. The Baking Pan/Drip Tray is a great addition to an already versatile appliance.

Step-By-Step Using It

Toast/Broil

When using the broil setting on your oven, it is important to keep an eye on your food to ensure that it does not overcook.

1.To broil, first preheat your oven and then place your food on the top wire rack. Make sure that the rack is centered so that the food cooks evenly.

2.Then set Temperature dial to Toast/Broil. Turn the oven timer dial to the specific required cooking time to turn the oven on and start broiling. The power light will be illuminated. The timer will ring when the cycle is complete and the oven will power off when the time expires.

3.To stop broiling, turn the ON/Oven Timer dial to the OFF position. For best results, check on your food frequently and use a specific meat thermometer to make sure that it has reached the desired internal temperature.

Bake

1.Before you begin baking, it is important to fit the baking pan or oven rack into the desired rack position.

2.Next, set the function dial to "Bake" and the temperature dial to the desired temperature. Then, turn the Oven Timer dial to the desired cooking time to start the oven and begin baking. It is recommended that you preheat the oven for 5 minutes before starting to bake; this should be incorporated into the total baking time. The power light will illuminate when the cycle starts, and the timer will ring once when the cycle is completed. Finally, the oven will power off automatically when the time expires.

3.If you need to stop baking before the cycle is complete, simply turn the ON/Oven Timer dial to the "off" position. By following these simple instructions, you can ensure that your baked goods come out perfectly every time.

Convection Bake

The Convection Bake setting on your oven can be used for a variety of different recipes.

1.To use this function, simply set the Temperature Dial to your desired cooking temperature and turn the ON/Oven Timer dial to the desired cooking time. It is recommended that you preheat your oven for 5 minutes before beginning to bake, so be sure to incorporate this into your total baking time.

2.Once you have set the timer, the power light will turn on and the oven will start baking. The timer will ring once when the cycle is complete and the oven will power off when the time expires. Depending on what you are baking, you may need to place your pan in Position 1 or 2. For chicken or other large items, the pan should be in Position 1.

3.If you need to stop the Convection Bake operation at any time, simply turn the ON/Oven Timer dial to the OFF position.

Warm

1.The best way to warm food is by using the Baking Pan or Oven Rack.

2.First, set the Temperature Dial to Warm. Then, set the Function Dial to Warm. After that, turn the ON/Oven Timer Dial to the desired warming time. The power light will illuminate and the timer will ring once the cycle is complete. When the time expires, the oven will power off.

3.Lastly, to stop warming, turn the ON/Oven Timer dial to the OFF position. By following these simple steps, you can have perfectly warmed food every time.

Toast

1.The first step is to fit the oven rack into position 2.

2.If you're only toasting one item, center it in the middle of the oven rack.

3.If you're toasting two items, also center them in the middle of the oven rack.

4.If you're toasting four items, space them evenly throughout the rack with two in front and two in back.

5.Lastly, if you're toasting six items, space them evenly throughout with three in front and three in back.

6.The next step is to set the function dial to "Toast." Then, set the temperature dial to "Toast/Broil." Finally, turn the ON/Toast Timer Dial to your desired shade setting within the marked settings. This will begin toasting your food.

7.The oven power light will illuminate and, once your toast is done, a timer will ring before turning off automatically.

8.If you want to stop toasting before the timer goes off, simply turn the ON/Toast Timer Dial to the OFF position.

Air Fry

1.The Air Fryer Basket must be placed onto the Baking Pan before beginning the Air Fry process. Make sure the Function Dial is set to Air Fry and the Temperature Dial is set to the desired temperature.

2.Then, turn the ON/Oven Timer dial to the desired cooking time to begin. The oven power light will illuminate and a timer will start. Once the cycle is complete, the timer will ring and the oven will power off automatically.

3.If you want to stop Air Frying before the cycle is complete, turn the ON/Oven Timer dial to the OFF position.

Tips for Using Accessories

This versatile appliance is used for a variety of cooking tasks. Here are some tips for getting the most out of your air fryer toaster oven:

1.Preheat the oven before use. This will help ensure evenly cooked food.

2.Cut food into small pieces to help it cook evenly.

3.Use the basket that comes with the oven to cook food in batches.

4.Shake or stir the basket occasionally during cooking to prevent sticking and ensure even cooking.

5.Keep an eye on food as it cooks, as cook times may be different depending on the size and type of food.

6.When using the Air Fry function, add oil to the food before cooking to help promote crispness.

7.Use the Warm function to quickly heat up leftovers or pre-cooked meals.

8.Clean the air fryer toaster oven after each use to prevent build-up of grease and food particles.

9.Store the air fryer toaster oven in a cool, dry place when not in use.

10.Follow all manufacturer's instructions carefully to prevent injury and damage to the appliance.

Cleaning and Caring for Cuisinart Air Fryer Oven

From time to time, your Cuisinart air fryer toaster oven will need a good cleaning. Whether it's because of spills or just general use, it's important to keep the appliance clean to prevent any build-up of grease or food particles. Luckily, cleaning the Cuisinart air fryer toaster oven is relatively simple and only takes a few minutes. Here are some steps you must follow:

1.Unplug the appliance and remove any food or debris.

2.Wipe down the inside and outside of the appliance with a damp cloth.

3.Use a mild soap if needed, but be sure to avoid any harsh chemicals or abrasives.

4.Dry the inside and outside of the appliance thoroughly with a clean towel.

5.Use a brush or toothpick to remove any stubborn bits of food or grease from the crevices and controls.

6.Replace any removable parts, such as the drip tray or racks.

7.Wipe down the heating element with a dry cloth. Do not use water on this part of the appliance.

8.Plug in the appliance and turn it on to its highest setting for one minute, then turn it off and let it cool completely. This will help to remove any residual soap or cleaners.

9.Once cooled, wipe down the interior one more time with a dry cloth before using it again.

10.Repeat this cleaning process as needed, depending on how often you use your Cuisinart air fryer toaster oven.

Maintenance

While it is relatively easy to use, there are a few things you should keep remember to maintain it. Here are some steps for maintaining your Cuisinart Air Fryer Toaster Oven:

1. Read the manual carefully before using the appliance. This will help you understand how to use it properly and avoid any damage.

2. Always clean the appliance after each use. This will prevent any build-up of grease or food particles, which can lead to problems down the line.

3. Use only mild soap and water to clean the appliance. Harsh chemicals can damage the finish or cause other problems.

4. Make sure the appliance is completely dry before storing it. Moisture can cause rusting or other damage.

5. Store the appliance in a cool, dry place when not in use. Extreme temperatures can damage the unit.

6. Do not use sharp objects on the interior of the appliance. This can scratch or damage the surface.

7. Do not place hot pots or pans directly on the exterior surface of the appliance. Use a trivet or other protective measure to avoid damage.

8. Do not attempt to repair or replace any part of the appliance yourself. This should only be done by a qualified technician only.

9. If you experience any problems with the appliance, contact customer service for assistance.

10. Keep these tips in mind and your Cuisinart Air Fryer Toaster Oven will provide years of trouble-free service!

Frequently Asked Questions & Notes

Are you curious about the Cuisinart Air Fryer Toaster Oven? Here are answers to 7 frequently asked questions about this appliance:

What is an air fryer toaster oven?

It is a toaster oven that uses hot air to cook food, resulting in a crispy finish.

How does it work?

The hot air circulates around the food, cooking it evenly.

What are the benefits of using an air fryer toaster oven?

It is a healthier way to cook food as there is no need for oil. Additionally, it is a versatile appliance as it can be used for baking, toasting and frying foods.

What types of food can be cooked in an air fryer toaster oven?

Many items such as chicken, fish, vegetables and potatoes can be cooked in this appliance.

What are the guidelines for cooking times?

Cooking times will vary depending on the type and size of the food being cooked. For example, chicken wings will take approximately 15 minutes while a whole chicken will take approximately 60 minutes.

What to do if I want to stop cooking midway?

Turn the ON/Oven Timer dial to the OFF position and the appliance will stop cooking immediately.

Can I leave the Cuisinart Air Fryer Toaster Oven unattended while it cooks?

No, it is not recommended as the appliance gets very hot during operation. Additionally, there is a risk of fire if food is left unattended in the appliance.

Notes

The Toaster Oven features a built-in air fryer with six presets, as well as a convection oven and a toaster. The appliance also has a stay-cool door handle, an automatic shut-off function, and a removable crumb tray.

⚠ To toast bread or bagels, place them on the wire rack in the center of the oven and select the desired doneness level by turning the ON/Toast Timer dial. The Cuisinart Air Fryer Toaster Oven will automatically shut off when the bread or bagels are done.

By following these simple tips, you'll be able to get the most out of your Cuisinart Air Fryer Toaster Oven.

4-Week Diet Plan

Week 1

Day 1:
Breakfast: Tofu Mushroom Omelet
Lunch: Butter Tomatoes
Snack: Tilapia Sticks
Dinner: Mustard Lamb Chops
Dessert: Chinese Beignet

Day 2:
Breakfast: Onion Tomato Quiche
Lunch: Kale with Oregano
Snack: Honey Veggies
Dinner: Stuffed Chicken Breast
Dessert: Sweet Avocado Bars

Day 3:
Breakfast: Cheese Egg Roll-Ups
Lunch: Basil Tomatoes
Snack: Cayenne Pickle Slices
Dinner: Lamb with Veggies
Dessert: Choco Mug Cake

Day 4:
Breakfast: Ground Sausage Casserole
Lunch: Brussels Sprout & Kale
Snack: Salmon Patties
Dinner: Mustard-Crusted Fillets
Dessert: Banana Walnut Cake

Day 5:
Breakfast: Spinach Bacon Muffins
Lunch: Broccoli Mix
Snack: Crunchy Peanuts
Dinner: Hone Chicken in Wine
Dessert: Jelly Raspberry Rolls

Day 6:
Breakfast: Rosemary Baked Eggs
Lunch: Asparagus and Broccoli
Snack: Parsley Italian Bread
Dinner: Salmon with Cauliflower
Dessert: Pecan Blueberry Cupcakes

Day 7:
Breakfast: Carrot Muffins
Lunch: Parmesan Radishes
Snack: Squash Bites
Dinner: Mint Lamb Patties
Dessert: Luscious Fruit Cake

Week 2

Day 1:
Breakfast: Beef Hot Dogs
Lunch: Cheese Broccoli
Snack: Almond Graham Crackers
Dinner: Lemon Chicken Thighs
Dessert: Filling Cheesecake

Day 2:
Breakfast: Lemon Salmon Quiche
Lunch: Celery Roots
Snack: Sausage Patties
Dinner: Hot Tandoori Lamb
Dessert: Chocolate Lava Cake

Day 3:
Breakfast: Bacon & Veggie Frittata
Lunch: Simple Asparagus
Snack: Easy Tasty Bratwursts
Dinner: Spiced Tilapia
Dessert: Cayenne Peanuts

Day 4:
Breakfast: Cream Egg & Ham
Lunch: Olives with Kale
Snack: Bacon-Wrapped Poppers
Dinner: Chicken Breast
Dessert: Fresh Cranberry Muffins

Day 5:
Breakfast: Sausage Frittata
Lunch: Honey Brussels Sprout
Snack: Yogurt Blueberry Muffins
Dinner: Salmon Patties
Dessert: Crispy Panko Bananas

Day 6:
Breakfast: Mozzarella Bacon Muffins
Lunch: Crunchy Masala Broccoli
Snack: Taco-Seasoned Beef Cups
Dinner: Lemon Rack of Lamb
Dessert: Cranberry Brownies

Day 7:
Breakfast: Onion Tomato Frittata
Lunch: Bacon with Green Beans
Snack: Bacon-Wrapped Scallops
Dinner: Rubbed Chicken Thigh
Dessert: Vanilla Puffed up

Day 1:
Breakfast: Trout Frittata
Lunch: Spicy Broccoli Florets
Snack: Beef Quinoa Meatballs
Dinner: Spiced Lamb Kebabs
Dessert: Lemon Blueberry Muffins

Day 2:
Breakfast: Cheese Ham Casserole
Lunch: Veggies with Basil
Snack: Basil Pesto Crackers
Dinner: Beer-Battered Cod
Dessert: Glazed Sweet Rolls

Day 3:
Breakfast: Eggs in Bread and Bacon Cups
Lunch: Spicy and Herby Eggplants
Snack: Cheese Broccoli Tots
Dinner: Spicy Chicken Breast
Dessert: Banana and Walnuts Bread

Day 4:
Breakfast: Bacon Spinach Quiche
Lunch: Cajun Peppers
Snack: Creole Almond Tomatoes
Dinner: Flavorful Shrimp
Dessert: Nutty Berry Slices

Day 5:
Breakfast: Veggie Sausage Frittata
Lunch: Avocado Olives Mix
Snack: Paprika Chickpeas
Dinner: Savory Chicken Legs
Dessert: Yummy Banana Muffins

Day 6:
Breakfast: Bread and Sausage Cups
Lunch: Mushrooms with Kale
Snack: Potato Fries
Dinner: Boneless Lamb Shoulder
Dessert: Chili Nut Mix

Day 7:
Breakfast: Lovely Macaroni Quiches
Lunch: Kale with Balsamic
Snack: Ham Potato Balls
Dinner: Avocado Chicken Mix
Dessert: Lemon Apple Pasty

Day 1:
Breakfast: Veggies Frittata with Scallion
Lunch: Cheese Green Beans
Snack: Coconut Cauliflower Tater Tots
Dinner: Crusted Salmon Patties
Dessert: Almond Zucchini Cake

Day 2:
Breakfast: Yogurt Turkey Casserole
Lunch: Butter Sweet Potatoes
Snack: Spinach Chicken Breast
Dinner: Crunchy Chicken Strips
Dessert: Salty Corn

Day 3:
Breakfast: Ham Veggies
Lunch: Spiced Carrots
Snack: Chat Banana Chips
Dinner: Seasoned Lamb Pieces
Dessert: Almond Cherry Bars

Day 4:
Breakfast: African Shakshuka
Lunch: Delicious Tomatoes & Broccoli
Snack: Fried Tomatoes
Dinner: Mutton Galette
Dessert: Syrup Banana Pieces

Day 5:
Breakfast: Tomato Spinach Frittata
Lunch: Curry Zucchini
Snack: Turmeric Cauliflower Patties
Dinner: Walnut Salmon
Dessert: Coconut Raspberry

Day 6:
Breakfast: Turkey Spinach
Lunch: Cheese Broccoli
Snack: Lemon Tofu Popcorns
Dinner: Chicken Vegetable Pie
Dessert: Cream Strawberry Pie

Day 7:
Breakfast: Broccoli Chicken Quiche
Lunch: Broccoli Salad
Snack: Vegetable Spring Rolls
Dinner: Spicy Tilapia Fillets
Dessert: Sweet Raspberry Roll

Chapter 1 Breakfast Recipes

Silken Tofu Omelet

Prep time: 15 minutes | Cook time: 10 minutes | Serves: 4

1 teaspoon arrowroot starch
2 teaspoons water
3 eggs
2 teaspoons fish sauce

1 teaspoon olive oil
Ground black pepper, to taste
8 ounces silken tofu, pressed and sliced

1. Dissolve arrowroot starch in water in a large bowl. 2. Add the eggs, fish sauce, tofu, oil and black pepper, and beat them well. Place tofu mixture in the Baking Pan and top with the egg mixture. 3. Insert the Baking Pan into rack Position 1. Set the Function Dial to Bake. Set Temperature Dial to 390 degrees F, and then turn the ON/Oven Timer dial to 10 minutes. 4. Let the Cuisinart Air Fryer Oven work. When done, cut the food into equal to sized wedges and serve hot.

Per serving: Calories 192; Fat 12g; Sodium 597 mg; Carbs 4.6g; Fiber 0.2g; Sugar 2.2g; Protein 16.4 g

Tofu Mushroom Omelet

Prep time: 15 minutes | Cook time: 35 minutes | Serves: 4

2 teaspoons canola oil
¼ of onion, chopped
1 garlic clove, minced
8 ounces silken tofu, pressed and sliced

3½ ounces fresh mushrooms, sliced
Salt and ground black pepper, as needed
3 eggs, beaten

1. Heat the oil in a skillet over medium heat; add the onion and garlic, and sauté them for about 4 to 5 minutes. 2. Add the mushrooms to the skillet, and sauté for about 4 to 5 minutes. 3. Remove the skillet from the heat, and stir in the tofu, salt and black pepper. 4. Place the tofu mixture into the Baking Pan and top with the beaten eggs. 5. Insert the Baking Pan into rack Position 1. Set the Function Dial to Bake. Set Temperature Dial to 355 degrees F, and then turn the ON/Oven Timer dial to 25 minutes. 6. Let the Cuisinart Air Fryer Oven work. When done, cut the food into equal to sized wedges and serve hot.

Per serving: Calories 224; Fat 14.5g; Sodium 214 mg; Carbs 6.6g; Fiber 0.9g; Sugar 3.4g; Protein 17.9 g

Cute Mushroom Frittatas

Prep time: 15 minutes | Cook time: 17 minutes | Serves: 3

1 tablespoon olive oil
½ of onion, sliced thinly
2 cups button mushrooms, sliced

3 eggs
Salt and ground black pepper, to taste
3 tablespoons feta cheese, crumbled

1. Heat the oil in a skillet over medium heat, and then cook the onion and mushroom with the oil for about 5 minutes. 2. Remove the skillet from the heat and set aside to cool slightly. Beat the eggs with salt and black pepper in a small bowl. 3. Divide the beaten eggs in 2 suitable greased ramekins, and top each with the mushroom mixture. 4. Place the ramekins in the Air Fryer Basket. Place the Air Fryer Basket onto the Baking Pan and insert into rack Position 2. Set the Function Dial to Air Fry. 5. Set Temperature Dial to 330 degrees F, and then turn the ON/Oven Timer dial to 12 minutes. 6. Let the Cuisinart Air Fryer Oven work. Serve hot.

Per serving: Calories 218; Fat 16.8g; Sodium 332 mg; Carbs 6g; Fiber 1.3g; Sugar 3.5g; Protein 12.8 g

Onion Tomato Frittata

Prep time: 10 minutes | Cook time: 30 minutes | Serves: 4

4 eggs

¼ cup onion, chopped

½ cup tomatoes, chopped

½ cup milk

1 cup Gouda cheese, shredded

Salt, to taste

1. Mix all the ingredients in the Baking Pan. 2. Insert the Baking Pan into rack Position 1. Set the Function Dial to Bake. 3. Set Temperature Dial to 340 degrees F, and then turn the ON/Oven Timer dial to 30 minutes. 4. Let the Cuisinart Air Fryer Oven work. Cut the frittata into 2 wedges after baking.

Per serving: Calories 247; Fat 16.1g; Sodium 417 mg; Carbs 7.3g; Fiber 0.9g; Sugar 5.2g; Protein 18.6 g

Broccoli Frittata with Shallot

Prep time: 15 minutes | Cook time: 36 minutes | Serves: 4

2 tablespoons olive oil

1 shallot, sliced thinly

2 garlic cloves, minced

4 cups broccoli, cut into florets

6 large eggs

¼ teaspoon red pepper flakes, crushed

Salt and ground black pepper, to taste

½ teaspoon fresh dill, minced

½ cup cream cheese, softened

1. Heat the oil in a skillet over medium heat, and stir-fry the shallot, broccoli and garlic for 5 to 6 minutes. 2. Transfer the broccoli mixture into a bowl. 3. Beat the eggs with red pepper flakes, salt and black peppers in another bowl; add the mushroom mixture and stir them to combine. 4. Place the egg mixture into the Baking Pan and sprinkle with the dill. Spread cream cheese over the egg mixture evenly. 5. Insert the Baking Pan into rack Position 1. Set the Function Dial to Bake. Set Temperature Dial to 330 degrees F, and then turn the ON/Oven Timer dial to 30 minutes. Let the Cuisinart Air Fryer Oven work. 6. When cooked, cut the frittata into equal to sized wedges and serve.

Per serving: Calories 290; Fat 24.8g; Sodium 236 mg; Carbs 5g; Fiber 0.8g; Sugar 1.9g; Protein 14.1 g

Veggies Frittata with Scallion

Prep time: 15 minutes | Cook time: 21 minutes | Serves: 4

½ teaspoon olive oil

4 fresh mushrooms, sliced

4 eggs

3 tablespoons heavy cream

Salt, to taste

4 tablespoons Cheddar cheese, grated

4 tablespoons fresh spinach, chopped

3 grape tomatoes, halved

2 tablespoons fresh mixed herbs, chopped

1 scallion, sliced

1. Heat the oil in a skillet over medium heat, and stir-fry the mushrooms in the skillet for 5 to 6 minutes. 2. Transfer the mushroom into a bowl. Beat the eggs with cream and salt in a bowl; add the mushroom and remaining ingredients and stir to combine. 3. Spread the mixture into the Baking Pan. Insert the Baking Pan into rack Position 1. Set the Function Dial to Bake. 4. Set Temperature Dial to 350 degrees F, and then turn the ON/Oven Timer dial to 15 minutes. Let the Cuisinart Air Fryer Oven work. 5. When cooked, cut the food into equal to sized wedges and serve.

Per serving: Calories 159; Fat 11.7g; Sodium 156 mg; Carbs 5.6g; Fiber 1.7g; Sugar 3.2g; Protein 9.1 g

Tomato Spinach Frittata

Prep time: 15 minutes | Cook time: 16 minutes | Serves: 4

¼ cup pancetta
½ of tomato, cubed
¼ cup fresh baby spinach

3 eggs
Salt and ground black pepper, to taste
¼ cup Parmesan cheese, grated

1. Heat a nonstick skillet over medium heat, and stir-fry the pancetta in it for about 5 minutes; add the tomato and spinach, and stir-fry them for 2 to 3 minutes. 2. Drain the grease from the skillet. Set aside to cool slightly. 3. Beat the eggs, salt and black pepper in a small bowl. Place the pancetta mixture in the Baking Pan and top with the eggs, followed by the cheese. 4. Insert the Baking Pan into rack Position 1. Set the Function Dial to Bake. Set Temperature Dial to 355 degrees F, and then turn the ON/Oven Timer dial to 8 minutes. 5. Let the Cuisinart Air Fryer Oven work. When cooked, cut the frittata into equal to sized wedges and serve.

Per serving: Calories 287; Fat 20.8g; Sodium 915 mg; Carbs 1.7g; Fiber 0.3g; Sugar 0.9g; Protein 23.1 g

Bacon & Veggie Frittata

Prep time: 15 minutes | Cook time: 16 minutes | Serves: 4

1 cooked bacon slice, chopped
6 cherry tomatoes, halved
6 fresh mushrooms, sliced
Salt and ground black pepper, to taste

3 eggs
1 tablespoon fresh parsley, chopped
¼ cup Parmesan cheese, grated

1. Beat the eggs in a bowl, and then stir in the parsley and cheese. 2. Mix the bacon, tomatoes, mushrooms, salt, and black pepper in the Baking Pan. 3. Insert the Baking Pan into rack Position 1. Set the Function Dial to Bake. Set Temperature Dial to 320 degrees F, and then turn the ON/Oven Timer dial to 16 minutes. 4. Top the bacon mixture with egg mixture evenly after 6 minutes of cooking. Let the Cuisinart Air Fryer Oven work. 5. When cooked, cut the frittata into equal to sized wedges and serve.

Per serving: Calories 228; Fat 15.5g; Sodium 608 mg; Carbs 3.5g; Fiber 0.9g; Sugar 2.1g; Protein 19.8 g

Veggie Sausage Frittata

Prep time: 15 minutes | Cook time: 30 minutes | Serves: 4

1 teaspoon butter
6 turkey sausage links, cut into small pieces
1 cup broccoli florets cut into small pieces
½ cup fresh spinach, chopped up
6 eggs

⅛ teaspoon hot sauce
2 tablespoons half to and to half
⅛ teaspoon garlic salt
Salt and ground black pepper, to taste
¾ cup Cheddar cheese, shredded

1. Melt the butter in a skillet over medium heat, and stir-fry the sausage in it for 7 to 8 minutes or until browned; add the broccoli, and stir-fry for about 3 to 4 minutes; add the spinach, and stir-fry for about 2 to 3 minutes. Turn off the heat and set aside to cool slightly. 2. Beat the eggs with half to and to half, hot sauce, garlic salt, salt and black pepper in a bowl until well combined, and then stir in the cheese. 3. Place the broccoli mixture in the Baking Pan and top with the egg mixture. 4. Insert the Baking Pan into rack Position 1. Set the Function Dial to Bake. Set Temperature Dial to 400 degrees F, and then turn the ON/Oven Timer dial to 15 minutes. Let the Cuisinart Air Fryer Oven work. 5. When cooked, cut the food into equal to sized wedges and serve hot.

Per serving: Calories 339; Fat 27.4g; Sodium 596 mg; Carbs 3.7g; Fiber 0.7g; Sugar 1.5g; Protein 19.6 g

Sausage Frittata

Prep time: 15 minutes | Cook time: 20 minutes | Serves: 4

¼ lb. cooked breakfast sausage, crumbled
½ cup Cheddar cheese, shredded
4 eggs, beaten lightly

2 scallions, chopped
Pinch of cayenne pepper

1. Combine the sausage, cheese, eggs, scallion and cayenne in a bowl. Place the mixture into the Baking Pan. 2. Insert the Baking Pan into rack Position 1. Set the Function Dial to Bake. 3. Set Temperature Dial to 360 degrees F, and then turn the ON/Oven Timer dial to 20 minutes. Let the Cuisinart Air Fryer Oven work. 4. When cooked, cut the frittata into equal to sized wedges and serve hot.
Per serving: Calories 437; Fat 32.4g; Sodium 726 mg; Carbs 2.2g; Fiber 0.4g; Sugar 1.2g; Protein 29.4 g

Trout Frittata

Prep time: 15 minutes | Cook time: 25 minutes | Serves: 6

1 tablespoon olive oil
1 onion, sliced
6 eggs
½ tablespoon horseradish sauce

2 tablespoons crème fraiche
2 hot-smoked trout fillets, chopped
¼ cup fresh dill, chopped

1. Heat the oil in a skillet over medium heat and cook the onion for about 4 to 5 minutes. Turn off the heat and set aside. 2. Mix the eggs, horseradish sauce, and crème fraiche in a bowl. 3. Transfer the cooked onion to the Baking Pan and top with the egg mixture, and then arrange the trout fillets on them. 4. Insert the Baking Pan into rack Position 1. Set the Function Dial to Bake. Set Temperature Dial to 320 degrees F, and then turn the ON/Oven Timer dial to 20 minutes. 5. Let the Cuisinart Air Fryer Oven work. 6. Cut the frittata into equal to sized wedges and serve with the garnishing of dill.
Per serving: Calories 258; Fat 15.7g; Sodium 141 mg; Carbs 5.1g; Fiber 1g; Sugar 1.8g; Protein 24.4 g

Lovely Macaroni Quiches

Prep time: 15 minutes | Cook time: 20 minutes | Serves: 4

1 short crust pastry
½ cup leftover macaroni n' cheese
2 tablespoons plain Greek yogurt
1 teaspoon garlic puree

11-ounce milk
2 large eggs
2 tablespoons Parmesan cheese, grated

1. Dust 4 ramekins with a little flour. Line the bottom of prepared ramekins with short crust pastry. 2. In a bowl, mix together macaroni, yogurt and garlic. Beat the eggs with milk in a small bowl. 3. Transfer the macaroni mixture between ramekins about ¾ full. Place the egg mixture over the macaroni mixture and top with the cheese evenly. 4. Transfer the ramekins to the Air Fryer Basket. Place the Air Fryer Basket onto the Baking Pan and insert into rack Position 2. Set the Function Dial to Air Fry. 5. Set Temperature Dial to 355 degrees F, and then turn the ON/Oven Timer dial to 20 minutes. 6. Serve hot.
Per serving: Calories 209; Fat 10.4g; Sodium 135 mg; Carbs 19.1g; Fiber 0.6g; Sugar 4.6g; Protein 9.6 g

Onion Tomato Quiche

Prep time: 15 minutes | Cook time: 30 minutes | Serves: 4

4 eggs
¼ cup onion, chopped
½ cup tomatoes, chopped

½ cup milk
1 cup Gouda cheese, shredded
Salt, to taste

1. Mix all the ingredients in the Baking Pan. 2. Insert the Baking Pan into rack Position 1. Set the Function Dial to Bake. Set Temperature Dial to 340 degrees F, and then turn the ON/Oven Timer dial to 30 minutes. 3. Let the Cuisinart Air Fryer Oven work. 4. Cut the quiche into equal to sized wedges and serve.
Per serving: Calories 247; Fat 16.1g; Sodium 417 mg; Carbs 7.3g; Fiber 0.9g; Sugar 5.2g; Protein 18.6 g

Broccoli Chicken Quiche

Prep time: 15 minutes | Cook time: 12 minutes | Serves: 4

½ of frozen ready to made pie crust
¼ tablespoon olive oil
1 small egg
3 tablespoons cheddar cheese, grated

1½ tablespoons whipping cream
Salt and black pepper, as needed
3 tablespoons boiled broccoli, chopped
2 tablespoons cooked chicken, chopped

1. Cut 1 (5-inch) round from the pie crust. Arrange the pie crust round in the Baking Pan and gently press in the bottom and sides. 2. In a bowl, mix together the egg, cheese, cream, salt, and black pepper. Pour the egg mixture over the dough base and top with the broccoli and chicken. 3. Insert the Baking Pan into rack Position 1. Set the Function Dial to Bake. Set Temperature Dial to 390 degrees F, and then turn the ON/Oven Timer dial to 12 minutes. 4. Let the Cuisinart Air Fryer Oven work. 5. Cut the quiche into equal to sized wedges and serve.
Per serving: Calories 197; Fat 15g; Sodium 184 mg; Carbs 7.4g; Fiber 0.4g; Sugar 0.9g; Protein 8.6 g

Lemon Salmon Quiche

Prep time: 15 minutes | Cook time: 20 minutes | Serves: 4

5½ ounces salmon fillet, chopped
Salt and ground black pepper, to taste
½ tablespoon fresh lemon juice
1 egg yolk
3½ tablespoons chilled butter

⅔ cup flour
1 tablespoon cold water
2 eggs
3 tablespoons whipping cream
1 scallion, chopped

1. In a bowl, mix together the salmon fillet, salt, black pepper and lemon juice. 2. In another bowl, add the egg yolk, butter, flour and water and mix until a dough forms. Place the dough onto a floured smooth surface and roll into about 7-inch round. 3. Place the dough in the Baking Pan and press firmly in the bottom and along the edges. Trim the excess edges. 4. Beat the eggs with cream, salt and black pepper in a small bowl. Place the cream mixture over the crust evenly and top with the salmon mixture, followed by the scallion. 5. Insert the Baking Pan into rack Position 1. Set the Function Dial to Bake. Set Temperature Dial to 355 degrees F, and then turn the ON/Oven Timer dial to 20 minutes. 6. Let the Cuisinart Air Fryer Oven work. Cut the quiche into equal to sized wedges and serve.
Per serving: Calories 592; Fat 39g; Sodium 331 mg; Carbs 33.8g; Fiber 1.4g; Sugar 0.8g; Protein 27.2 g

Bacon Spinach Quiche

Prep time: 15 minutes | Cook time: 10 minutes | Serves: 4

2 cooked bacon slices, chopped
½ cup fresh spinach, chopped
¼ cup mozzarella cheese, shredded
½ cup Parmesan cheese, shredded

2 tablespoons milk
2 dashes Tabasco sauce
Salt and ground black pepper, to taste

1. In a bowl, mix all ingredients. Transfer the mixture into the Baking Pan. 2. Insert the Baking Pan into rack Position 1. Set the Function Dial to Bake. Set Temperature Dial to 320 degrees F, and then turn the ON/ Oven Timer dial to 10 minutes. 3. Let the Cuisinart Air Fryer Oven work. 4. Cut the quiche into equal to sized wedges and serve hot.
Per serving: Calories 130; Fat 9.3g; Sodium 561 mg; Carbs 1.1g; Fiber 0.1g; Sugar 0.4g; Protein 10 g

Spicy Sausage Casserole

Prep time: 15 minutes | Cook time: 19 minutes | Serves: 8

1 tablespoon olive oil
½ lb. spicy ground sausage
¾ cup yellow onion, chopped
5 fresh mushrooms, sliced

8 eggs, beaten
½ teaspoon garlic salt
¾ cup Cheddar cheese, shredded and divided
¼ cup Alfredo sauce

1. Heat the oil in a skillet over medium heat and cook the sausage and onions for about 4 to 5 minutes. 2. Add the mushrooms and cook for about 6 to 7 minutes. 3. Drain the grease from the skillet. In a bowl, add the sausage mixture, beaten eggs, garlic salt, ½ cup of cheese and Alfredo sauce and stir to combine. 4. Place the sausage mixture into the Baking Pan. Insert the Baking Pan into rack Position 2. Set the Function Dial to Bake. Set Temperature Dial to 390 degrees F, and then turn the ON/Oven Timer dial to 12 minutes. 5. Let the Cuisinart Air Fryer Oven work. 6. Cut into equal to sized wedges and serve with the topping of remaining cheese.
Per serving: Calories 319; Fat 24.5g; Sodium 698 mg; Carbs 5g; Fiber 0.5g; Sugar 1.5g; Protein 19.7 g

Ground Sausage Casserole

Prep time: 15 minutes | Cook time: 25 minutes | Serves: 8

1 teaspoon olive oil
1 lb. ground sausage
1 green bell pepper, seeded and chopped
¼ cup onion, chopped

8 eggs, beaten
½ cup Colby Jack cheese, shredded
1 teaspoon fennel seed
½ teaspoon garlic salt

1. Heat the oil in a skillet over medium heat and cook the sausage for about 4 to 5 minutes. Add the bell pepper and onion and cook for about 4 to 5 minutes. 2. Turn off the heat and transfer the sausage mixture into a bowl to cool slightly. 3. In the Baking Pan, place the sausage mixture and top with the cheese, followed by the beaten eggs, fennel seed and garlic salt. 4. Insert the Baking Pan into rack Position 1. Set the Function Dial to Bake. Set Temperature Dial to 390 degrees F, and then turn the ON/Oven Timer dial to 15 minutes. 5. Let the Cuisinart Air Fryer Oven work. 6. Cut into equal to sized wedges and serve hot.
Per serving: Calories 394; Fat 1.1g; Sodium 709 mg; Carbs 3.1g; Fiber 0.5g; Sugar 1.7g; Protein 24.4 g

Yogurt Turkey Casserole

Prep time: 10 minutes | Cook time: 25 minutes | Serves: 6

6 eggs
½ cup plain Greek yogurt
½ cup cooked turkey meat, chopped

Salt and ground black pepper, to taste
½ cup sharp Cheddar cheese, shredded

1. Beat the egg with yogurt in a bowl; add the remaining ingredients and stir to combine. 2. In the greased Baking Pan, place the egg mixture. 3. Insert the Baking Pan into rack Position 1. Set the Function Dial to Bake. Set Temperature Dial to 375 degrees F, and then turn the ON/Oven Timer dial to 25 minutes. 4. Let the Cuisinart Air Fryer Oven work. 5. Cut into equal to sized wedges and serve.

Per serving: Calories 203; Fat 12.5g; Sodium 253 mg; Carbs 2.9g; Fiber 0g; Sugar 0.4g; Protein 18.7 g

Cheese Ham Casserole

Prep time: 15 minutes | Cook time: 37 minutes | Serves: 6

1½ tablespoons olive oil
½ of large onion, chopped
24 ounces frozen hashbrowns
3 eggs

2 tablespoons milk
Salt and ground black pepper, to taste
½ lb. ham, chopped
¼ cup Cheddar cheese, shredded

1. Heat the oil in a skillet over medium heat and sauté the onion for about 4 to 5 minutes. Turn off the heat and transfer the onion into a bowl. 2. Add the hashbrowns and mix well. Place the mixture into the Baking Pan. 3. Insert the Baking Pan into rack Position 1. Set the Function Dial to Bake. Set Temperature Dial to 350 degrees F, and then turn the ON/Oven Timer dial to 32 minutes. 4. Let the Cuisinart Air Fryer Oven work. Meanwhile, in a bowl, add the eggs, milk, salt and black pepper and beat well. 5. After 15 minutes of cooking, place the egg mixture over the hashbrown mixture evenly and top with the ham. 6. After 30 minutes of cooking, sprinkle the casserole with the cheese. Cut into equal to sized wedges and serve.

Per serving: Calories 540; Fat 29.8g; Sodium 1110 mg; Carbs 51.5g; Fiber 5.3g; Sugar 3.2g; Protein 16.7 g

Cream Egg & Ham

Prep time: 15 minutes | Cook time: 13 minutes | Serves: 4

2 teaspoons unsalted butter, softened
2 ounces ham, sliced thinly
4 large eggs
Salt and ground black pepper, to taste

2 tablespoons heavy cream
⅛ teaspoon smoked paprika
3 tablespoons Parmesan cheese, grated
2 teaspoons fresh chives, minced

1. Spread butter in the bottom of the Baking Pan. Arrange the ham slices over the butter. 2. In a bowl, add 1egg, salt, black pepper and cream and beat until smooth. Place the egg mixture over the ham slices evenly. 3. Carefully, crack the remaining eggs on top and sprinkle with paprika, salt, black pepper, cheese and chives evenly. 4. Insert the Baking Pan into rack Position 1. Set the Function Dial to Bake. Set Temperature Dial to 320 degrees F, and then turn the ON/Oven Timer dial to 13 minutes. 5. Let the Cuisinart Air Fryer Oven work. 6. Cut into equal to sized wedges and serve.

Per serving: Calories 302; Fat 23.62g; Sodium 685 mg; Carbs 2.4g; Fiber 0.5g; Sugar 0.8g; Protein 20.7 g

Turkey Spinach

Prep time: 15 minutes | Cook time: 23 minutes | Serves: 4

1 tablespoon unsalted butter
1 lb. fresh baby spinach
4 eggs

7 ounces cooked turkey, chopped
4 teaspoons milk
Salt and ground black pepper, to taste

1. In a skillet, melt the butter over medium heat and cook the spinach for about 2 to 3 minutes or until just wilted. Turn off the heat and transfer the spinach into a bowl. Set aside to cool slightly. 2. Divide the spinach into 4 greased ramekins, followed by the turkey. Crack 1 egg into each ramekin and drizzle with milk. 3. Sprinkle with salt and black pepper, and then place the ramekins in the Air Fryer Basket. 4. Place the Air Fryer Basket onto the Baking Pan and insert into rack Position 2. Set the Function Dial to Air Fry. Set Temperature Dial to 355 degrees F, and then turn the ON/Oven Timer dial to 20 minutes. 5. Let the Cuisinart Air Fryer Oven work. 6. Serve hot.
Per serving: Calories 201; Fat 10.3g; Sodium 248 mg; Carbs 4.7g; Fiber 2.5g; Sugar 1.1g; Protein 23.5 g

Ham Veggies

Prep time: 15 minutes | Cook time: 15 minutes | Serves: 4

1 teaspoon olive oil
6 small button mushrooms, quartered
6 cherry tomatoes, halved
4 slices shaved ham
2 tablespoons spinach, chopped

1 cup cheddar cheese, shredded
2 eggs
1 tablespoon fresh rosemary, chopped
Salt and ground black pepper, to taste

1. Heat the oil in a skillet over medium heat and cook the mushrooms for about 6 to 7 minutes. Turn off the heat and set aside to cool slightly. 2. In a bowl, mix together the mushrooms, tomatoes, ham and greens. Place half of the vegetable mixture in the Air Fryer Basket and top with half of the cheese. 3. Repeat the layers once. Make 2 wells in the mixture. 4. Place the Air Fryer Basket onto the Baking Pan and insert into rack Position 2. Set the Function Dial to Air Fry. Set Temperature Dial to 390 degrees F, and then turn the ON/Oven Timer dial to 8 minutes. 5. Let the Cuisinart Air Fryer Oven work. Serve hot.
Per serving: Calories 424; Fat 30.7g; Sodium 1140 mg; Carbs 7g; Fiber 2.3g; Sugar 2.2g; Protein 31 g

Cheese Egg Roll-Ups

Prep time: 10 minutes | Cook time: 23 minutes | Serves: 4

12 slices sugar to free bacon.
½ medium green bell pepper; seeded and chopped
6 large eggs.
¼ cup chopped onion

1 cup shredded sharp cheddar cheese.
½ cup mild salsa, for dipping
2 tablespoons unsalted butter.

1. Melt the butter in a medium skillet over medium heat. Add onion and pepper to the skillet and sauté them for 3 minutes until fragrant and onions are translucent. 2. Whisk eggs in a small bowl and pour into skillet. Scramble eggs with onions and peppers for 5 minutes until fluffy and fully cooked. Remove from heat and set aside. 3. On the work surface, place 3 slices of bacon side by side, overlapping about ¼-inch. Place ¼ cup scrambled eggs in a heap on the side closest to you and sprinkle ¼ cup cheese on top of the eggs. 4. Tightly roll the bacon around the eggs and secure the seam with a toothpick if necessary. Place each roll into the Air Fryer Basket. 5. Place the Air Fryer Basket onto the Baking Pan and insert into rack Position 2. Set the Function Dial to Air Fry. Set Temperature Dial to 350 degrees F, and then turn the ON/Oven Timer dial to 15 minutes. 6. Let the Cuisinart Air Fryer Oven work. Rotate the rolls halfway through the cooking time. 7. Serve immediately with salsa for dipping.
Per serving: Calories 460; Fat 31,7 g; Sodium 643 mg; Carbs 6.1g; Fiber 0.8g; Sugar 1.3g; Protein 28.2 g

Bread and Sausage Cups

Prep time: 10 minutes | Cook time: 22 minutes | Serves: 4

¼ cup cream

3 eggs

2 cooked sausages, sliced

1 bread slice, cut into sticks

¼ cup mozzarella cheese, grated

1. In a bowl, add the cream and eggs and beat well. Transfer the egg mixture into ramekins. 2. Place the sausage slices and bread sticks around the edges and gently push them in the egg mixture. Sprinkle with the cheese evenly. 3. Place the ramekins into rack Position 1. Set the Function Dial to Bake. Set Temperature Dial to 355 degrees F, and then turn the ON/Oven Timer dial to 22 minutes. Let the Cuisinart Air Fryer Oven work. 4. Serve warm.

Per serving: Calories 229; Fat 18.6g; Sodium 360 mg; Carbs 3.9g; Fiber 0.1g; Sugar 1.3g; Protein 15.2 g

Eggs in Bread and Bacon Cups

Prep time: 10 minutes | Cook time: 15 minutes | Serves: 4

4 bacon slices

4 bread slices

1 scallion, chopped

2 tablespoons bell pepper, seeded and chopped

1½ tablespoons mayonnaise

4 eggs

1. Grease 6 cups muffin tin with cooking spray. Line the sides of each prepared muffin cup with 1 bacon slice. Cut bread slices with round cookie cutter. 2. Arrange the bread slice in the bottom of each muffin cup. Top each with scallion, bell pepper and mayonnaise evenly. 3. Carefully, crack 1 egg in each muffin cup. Place the muffin cups in the Air Fryer Basket. 4. Place the Air Fryer Basket onto the Baking Pan and insert into rack Position 2. Set the Function Dial to Air Fry. Set Temperature Dial to 375 degrees F, and then turn the ON/Oven Timer dial to 15 minutes. 5. Let the Cuisinart Air Fryer Oven work. Serve warm.

Per serving: Calories 298; Fat 20.7g; Sodium 829 mg; Carbs 10.1g; Fiber 1.1g; Sugar 3.8g; Protein 17.6 g

Spinach and Mozzarella Muffins

Prep time: 10 minutes | Cook time: 10 minutes | Serves: 2

2 large eggs

2 tablespoons half to and to half

2 tablespoons frozen spinach, thawed

4 teaspoons mozzarella cheese, grated

Salt and ground black pepper, to taste

1. Grease 2 ramekins. In each prepared ramekin, crack 1 egg. 2. Divide the half to and to half, spinach, cheese, salt and black pepper and each ramekin and gently stir to combine, without breaking the yolks. 3. Place the ramekins in the Air Fryer Basket. Place the Air Fryer Basket onto the Baking Pan and insert into rack Position 2. Set the Function Dial to Air Fry. 4. Set Temperature Dial to 330 degrees F, and then turn the ON/Oven Timer dial to 10 minutes. 5. Let the Cuisinart Air Fryer Oven work. Serve warm.

Per serving: Calories 251; Fat 16.7g; Sodium 495 mg; Carbs 3.1g; Fiber 0g; Sugar 0.4g; Protein 22.8 g

Spinach Bacon Muffins

Prep time: 10 minutes | Cook time: 17 minutes | Serves: 6

6 eggs
½ cup milk
Salt and ground black pepper, to taste

1 cup fresh spinach, chopped
4 cooked bacon slices, crumbled

1. In a bowl, add the eggs, milk, salt and black pepper and beat until well combined. Add the spinach and stir to combine. 2. Divide the spinach mixture into 6 greased cups of an egg bite mold evenly. Transfer the cups to the Air Fryer Basket. 3. Place the Air Fryer Basket onto the Baking Pan and insert into rack Position 2. Set the Function Dial to Air Fry. Set Temperature Dial to 325 degrees F, and then turn the ON/Oven Timer dial to 17 minutes. 4. Let the Cuisinart Air Fryer Oven work. Top the dish with bacon pieces and serve warm.
Per serving: Calories 179; Fat 12.9g; Sodium 549 mg; Carbs 1.8g; Fiber 0.1g; Sugar 1.3g; Protein 13.5 g

Mozzarella Bacon Muffins

Prep time: 10 minutes | Cook time: 18 minutes | Serves: 6

6 bacon slices
6 eggs
6 tablespoons cream

3 tablespoon mozzarella cheese, shredded
¼ teaspoon dried basil, crushed

1. Lightly grease 6 cups of a silicone muffin tin. Line each prepared muffin cup with 1 bacon slice. 2. Crack 1 egg into each muffin cup and top with cream. Sprinkle with cheese and basil. 3. Place the muffin tin into rack Position 2. Set the Function Dial to Air Fry. Set Temperature Dial to 350 degrees F, and then turn the ON/Oven Timer dial to 18 minutes. Let the Cuisinart Air Fryer Oven work. 4. Serve warm.
Per serving: Calories 156; Fat 10g; Sodium 516 mg; Carbs 2.3g; Fiber 0.4g; Sugar 0.6g; Protein 14.3 g

Carrot Muffins

Prep time: 15 minutes | Cook time: 7 minutes | Serves: 6

For Muffins:
¼ cup whole to wheat flour
¼ cup all to purpose flour
½ teaspoon baking powder
⅛ teaspoon baking soda
½ teaspoon dried parsley, crushed
½ teaspoon salt
For Topping:
7 ounces Parmesan cheese, grated

½ cup plain yogurt
1 teaspoon vinegar
1 tablespoon vegetable oil
3 tablespoons cottage cheese, grated
1 carrot, peeled and grated
2 to 4 tablespoons water

¼ cup walnuts, chopped

1. Mix the flours, baking powder, baking soda, parsley, and salt in a large bowl. 2. In another large bowl, mix well the yogurt, and vinegar. Add the remaining ingredients except water and beat them well. 3. Make a well in the center of the yogurt mixture. Slowly add the flour mixture in the well and mix until well combined. 4. Place the mixture into lightly greased muffin molds evenly and top with the Parmesan cheese and walnuts. 5. Transfer the molds in the Air Fryer Basket. Place the Air Fryer Basket onto the Baking Pan and insert into rack Position 2. Set the Function Dial to Air Fry. 6. Set Temperature Dial to 355 degrees F, and then turn the ON/Oven Timer dial to 7 minutes. Let the Cuisinart Air Fryer Oven work. 7. Serve.
Per serving: Calories 292; Fat 13.1g; Sodium 579 mg; Carbs 27.2g; Fiber 1.5g; Sugar 2g; Protein 17.7 g

Jalapeno Potato Hash

Prep time: 15 minutes | Cook time: 25 minutes | Serves: 4

2 cups water
5 russet potatoes, peeled and cubed
½ tablespoon olive oil
½ of onion, chopped
½ of jalapeño, chopped
1 green bell pepper, seeded and chopped

¼ teaspoon dried oregano, crushed
¼ teaspoon garlic powder
¼ teaspoon ground cumin
¼ teaspoon red chili powder
Salt and black pepper, as needed

1. In a large bowl, add the water and potatoes and set aside for about 30 minutes. Drain well and pat dry with paper towels. 2. In a bowl, add the potatoes and oil and toss to coat well. Arrange the potato cubes into the Air Fryer Basket. 3. Place the Air Fryer Basket onto the Baking Pan and insert into rack Position 2. Set the Function Dial to Air Fry. Set Temperature Dial to 330 degrees F, and then turn the ON/Oven Timer dial to 5 minutes. 4. Let the Cuisinart Air Fryer Oven work. Transfer the cooked potatoes onto a plate. 5. In a bowl, add the potatoes and remaining ingredients and toss to coat well. Arrange the veggie mixture in the Air Fryer Basket. 6. Place the Air Fryer Basket onto the Baking Pan and insert into rack Position 2. Set the Function Dial to Air Fry. Set Temperature Dial to 390 degrees F, and then turn the ON/Oven Timer dial to 20 minutes. 7. Let the Cuisinart Air Fryer Oven work. Serve hot.
Per serving: Calories 216; Fat 2.2g; Sodium 58 mg; Carbs 45.7g; Fiber 7.2g; Sugar 5.2g; Protein 5 g

Rosemary Baked Eggs

Prep time: 10 minutes. | Cook time: 13 minutes. | Serves: 2

4 eggs
2 teaspoons olive oil
1 teaspoon rosemary

1 teaspoon basil
½ teaspoon garlic powder
Sea salt and ground black pepper, to taste

1. Brush two ramekins with olive oil. Then crack two eggs into each ramekin. 2. Season the eggs with rosemary, basil, garlic powder, salt, and pepper. Place the ramekins on the Baking Pan in the center position. 3. Insert the Baking Pan into rack Position 1. Set the Function Dial to Bake. Set Temperature Dial to 350 degrees F, and then turn the ON/Oven Timer dial to 13 minutes. 4. Let the Cuisinart Air Fryer Oven work. Serve warm.
Per serving: Calories 169; Fat 12g; Sodium 430mg; Carbs 1.2g; Sugar 0.6g; Fiber 0.7g; Protein 11.2g

Typical Blueberry Muffins

Prep time: 10 minutes. | Cook time: 20 minutes. | Serves: 6

1 cup all to purpose flour
1 cup coconut flour
1 teaspoon baking powder
¼ teaspoon salt
1 cup granulated; Sugar
½ cup coconut oil, at room temperature

2 large eggs, whisked
½ teaspoon cinnamon powder
1 teaspoon vanilla paste
½ cup milk
2 cups fresh or frozen blueberries

1. In a mixing bowl, stir together the dry ingredients. In a separate bowl, thoroughly combine the wet ingredients. 2. Add the wet mixture to the dry ingredients and stir just until moistened. Gently fold in the blueberries. Spoon the batter into a parchment to lined muffin tin. Place the muffin tin in the Baking Pan. 3. Insert the Baking Pan into rack Position 1. Set the Function Dial to Bake. Set Temperature Dial to 330 degrees F, and then turn the ON/Oven Timer dial to 20 minutes. 4. Let the Cuisinart Air Fryer Oven work. Serve.
Per serving: Calories 410; Fat 25.2g; Sodium 384mg; Carbs 42.2g; Sugar 0.8g; Fiber 0.7g; Protein 5.5g

Bacon and Cheese Toasted Sandwich

Prep time: 10 minutes. | Cook time: 9 minutes. | Serves: 1

2 (1-inch thick) slices bread

1 (1-ounce) slice cheese

1 (1-ounce) slice bacon

1. Place the bacon on the Air Fryer Basket. Place the Air Fryer Basket onto the Baking Pan and insert into rack Position 2. Set the Function Dial to Air Fry. 2. Set Temperature Dial to 390 degrees F, and then turn the ON/Oven Timer dial to 6 minutes. Let the Cuisinart Air Fryer Oven work. 3. Place the fried bacon on a paper towel and reserve. Assemble the bread slices with the cheese and reserved bacon; you can use a toothpick to keep the sandwich together. 4. Place them in the Baking Pan. Insert the Baking Pan into rack Position 1. Set the Function Dial to Bake. Set Temperature Dial to 350 degrees F, and then turn the ON/Oven Timer dial to 3 minutes. 5. Cook them until crispy and golden brown on top. Serve immediately.

Per serving: Calories 301; Fat 18.2g; Sodium 502mg; Carbs 22.5g; Sugar 1.2g; Fiber 0.7g; Protein 11.5g

Beef Hot Dogs

Prep time: 10 minutes. | Cook time: 15 minutes. | Serves: 2

2 beef sausages

2 hot dog buns

2 tablespoons tomato ketchup

2 tablespoons Dijon mustard

1. Place the sausage on the Air Fryer Basket. Place the Air Fryer Basket onto the Baking Pan and insert into rack Position 2. Set the Function Dial to Air Fry. 2. Set Temperature Dial to 360 degrees F, and then turn the ON/Oven Timer dial to 15 minutes. 3. Let the Cuisinart Air Fryer Oven work. 4. Serve the warm sausages on hot dog buns, garnished with ketchup and mustard. Enjoy!

Per serving: Calories 521; Fat 33.9g; Sodium 502mg; Carbs 33.1g; Sugar 1.1g; Fiber 0.7g; Protein 20.6g

African Shakshuka

Prep time: 10 minutes. | Cook time: 15 minutes. | Serves: 4

2 teaspoons olive oil

6 eggs

1 small onion, peeled, halved and sliced

½ teaspoon fresh garlic, pressed

1 bell pepper, deseeded and sliced

1 chili pepper, deseeded and sliced

1 medium tomato, chopped

½ cup tomato soup

Sea salt and ground black pepper, to taste

1 teaspoon saffron (optional)

1. Grease the Baking Pan with olive oil and set it aside. 2. Whisk the eggs in a large mixing bowl until frothy. Stir in the remaining ingredients. 3. Pour the egg mixture into the pan. Insert the Baking Pan into rack Position 1. Set the Function Dial to Bake. 4. Set Temperature Dial to 350 degrees F, and then turn the ON/Oven Timer dial to 15 minutes. 5. Let the Cuisinart Air Fryer Oven work. Serve.

Per serving: Calories 150; Fat 8.7g; Sodium 427mg; Carbs 7.4g; Sugar 1.4g; Fiber 0.7g; Protein 9.6g

Chapter 2 Snack and Appetizer Recipes

Almond Cauliflower Chunks

Prep time: 10 minutes | Cook time: 15 minutes | Serves: 4

1 cauliflower head, diced into chunks
½ cup unsweetened almond milk
1 tbsp. mayo
¼ cup all to purpose flour
¾ cup almond meal
¼ cup almond meal

1 tsp. onion powder
1 tsp. garlic powder
1 tsp. of sea salt
½ tsp. paprika
Pinch of black pepper
Cooking oil spray

1. In a mixing bowl, toss the cauliflower with the remaining ingredients, and then put them to the Baking Pan; coat them with frying oil. 2. Insert the Baking Pan into rack Position 1. Set the Function Dial to Bake. Set Temperature Dial to 400 degrees F, and then turn the ON/Oven Timer dial to 15 minutes. 3. Let the Cuisinart Air Fryer Oven work. Once done, serve and enjoy.
Per Serving: Calories 180; Fat 11g; Sodium 517mg; Carbs 15.7g; Fiber 4.7g; Sugar 3.3g; Protein 7.4g

Lemon Tofu Popcorns

Prep time: 15 minutes | Cook time: 15 minutes | Serves: 4

2 cups tofu, diced
3 to ¾ cups vegetable broth, divided
2 garlic cloves, mashed
1 tsp. salt
1-inch cube ginger, grated
½ cup all to purpose flour

½ cup of corn starch
1 cup panko breadcrumbs
1 tbsp. garlic powder
1 tbsp. lemon pepper
½ tsp. salt

1. In a large mixing bowl, combine tofu, ginger, salt, and garlic. Soak them for 20 minutes with 3 cups of broth. 2. In a mixing bowl, whisk together wheat flour, cornstarch, and ¾ cup broth until smooth. Toss the tofu cubes in the flour batter after removing them from the milk. 3. Arrange tofu cubes into the Air Fryer Basket. Place the Air Fryer Basket onto the Baking Pan and insert into rack Position 2. Set the Function Dial to Air Fry. 4. Set Temperature Dial to 390 degrees F, and then turn the ON/Oven Timer dial to 15 minutes. 5. Let the Cuisinart Air Fryer Oven work. Turn the food halfway through. 6. Once done, serve and enjoy.
Per Serving: Calories 335; Fat 7.3g; Sodium 1450mg; Carbs 51.7g; Fiber 4.7g; Sugar 2.5g; Protein 19.4g

Easy Tasty Bratwursts

Prep time: 10 minutes | Cook time: 12 minutes | Serves: 4

1 pack bratwursts

1. Arrange bratwursts into the Baking Pan. Insert the Baking Pan into rack Position 1. Set the Function Dial to Bake. 2. Set Temperature Dial to 350 degrees F, and then turn the ON/Oven Timer dial to 10 minutes. Let the Cuisinart Air Fryer Oven work. 3. Once done, serve and enjoy.
Per Serving: Calories 71; Fat 6.3g; Sodium 180mg; Carbs 0.7g; Fiber 0g; Sugar 0g; Protein 2.9g

Turmeric Cauliflower Patties

Prep time: 10 minutes | Cook time: 20 minutes | Serves: 4

3 large eggs
3 cups cauliflower florets
½ cup all to purpose flour
3 tbsp. wheat flour
1 tsp. coconut oil (melted)

½ tsp. garlic powder
½ tsp. turmeric
½ tsp. parsley
Salt & pepper to taste
Cooking oil spray

1. In a food processor, grate the cauliflower, then add the parsley, turmeric, garlic powder, and wheat flour. 2. Mix thoroughly after whisking in the eggs and coconut oil. This cauliflower mixture should yield 4 patties. 3. Arrange patties into the Air Fryer Basket. Place the Air Fryer Basket onto the Baking Pan and insert into rack Position 2. Set the Function Dial to Air Fry. Set Temperature Dial to 350 degrees F, and then turn the ON/Oven Timer dial to 20 minutes. 4. Let the Cuisinart Air Fryer Oven work. Turn the food halfway through. Once done, serve and enjoy.
Per Serving: Calories 150; Fat 5.3g; Sodium 76mg; Carbs 18.7g; Fiber 2.7g; Sugar 2.2g; Protein 8.1g

Tilapia Sticks

Prep time: 10 minutes | Cook time: 15 minutes | Serves: 4

4 frozen tilapia fillets, cut into sticks
1 cup all to purpose flour
2 large eggs, beaten
For Serving:
1 lemon, cut in wedges
Tartar sauce

1 ½ cups seasoned panko breadcrumbs
1 tbsp. kosher salt

Ketchup

1. Dredge the tilapia sticks in flour with salt, then dip them in the egg, and finally coat them with the crumb mixture. 2. Place the coated sticks in the Air Fryer Basket. Place the Air Fryer Basket onto the Baking Pan and insert into rack Position 2. Set the Function Dial to Air Fry. 3. Set Temperature Dial to 390 degrees F, and then turn the ON/Oven Timer dial to 12 minutes. Let the Cuisinart Air Fryer Oven work. 4. Turn the food halfway through. Once done, serve and enjoy.
Per Serving: Calories 415; Fat 10.6g; Sodium 2350mg; Carbs 49.7g; Fiber 2.3g; Sugar 0.2g; Protein 30.4g

Bacon-Wrapped Scallops

Prep time: 10 minutes | Cook time: 12 minutes | Serves: 9

½ cup mayonnaise
2 tbsp. Sriracha sauce
1-pound bay scallops
1 pinch coarse salt

1 pinch freshly cracked black pepper
4 slices bacon, cut into three pieces
Olive oil cooking; Spray

1. Add Sriracha sauce and mayonnaise to a bowl and set aside. Place the scallops on a work surface and dry them. 2. Season them with salt and black pepper, then wrap a third of a bacon slice around each scallop and fasten with a toothpick. 3. Arrange scallops into the Air Fryer Basket. Place the Air Fryer Basket onto the Baking Pan and insert into rack Position 2. Set the Function Dial to Air Fry. 4. Set Temperature Dial to 390 degrees F, and then turn the ON/Oven Timer dial to 7 minutes. 5. Let the Cuisinart Air Fryer Oven work. Turn the food halfway through. Once done, serve and enjoy.
Per Serving: Calories 177; Fat 12.3g; Sodium 422mg; Carbs 4.7g; Fiber 0g; Sugar 1.1g; Protein 11.4g

Almond Graham Crackers

Prep time: 10 minutes | Cook time: 45 minutes | Serves: 8

2 cups self to rising; flour
1 cup almond flour
1 teaspoon baking; powder
½ cup butter, softened

½ cup packed brown sugar
⅓ cup honey
1 teaspoon vanilla extract
½ cup coconut milk

1. Separately sieve self to rising flour, almond flour, baking powder, and baking powder. Butter, brown sugar, and honey in a medium container, mix softly and loosely. 2. Alternate adding the sifted ingredients with the milk and vanilla extract. Cover the dough and set it aside to chill overnight. Make quarters out of the cold dough. 3. Quarterly, roll out the dough into a 5 x 15-inch rectangle on a well to floured board. Cut the dough into rectangles. 4. Place rectangles on baking sheets that haven't been greased. Draw a line in the center and use a fork to click it. 5. Sprinkle a mixture of sugar and cinnamon on the biscuits before baking for a cinnamon biscuit. Arrange cinnamon biscuit to the Baking Pan. 6. Insert the Baking Pan into rack Position 1. Set the Function Dial to Bake. Set Temperature Dial to 350 degrees F, and then turn the ON/ Oven Timer dial to 15 minutes. 7. Let the Cuisinart Air Fryer Oven work. Once done, serve and enjoy.
Per Serving: Calories 396; Fat 22.1g; Sodium 127mg; Carbs 40.7g; Fiber 8.7g; Sugar 22.5g; Protein 3.4g

Chicken Fillets with Italian Seasoning

Prep time: 10 minutes | Cook time: 15 minutes | Serves: 4

4 ounces garlic and herb cream cheese
Salt and pepper to taste
2 teaspoons dried Italian seasoning

Olive oil as needed
2 chicken breast fillets

1. Brush the chicken with oil and set aside. Season them with salt, pepper, and Italian seasoning, and top the meat with cream cheese with garlic and herbs. 2. Carefully roll up the chicken. Arrange chicken into the Baking Pan. Insert the Baking Pan into rack Position 1. Set the Function Dial to Bake. 3. Set Temperature Dial to 370 degrees F, and then turn the ON/Oven Timer dial to 7 minutes. 4. Let the Cuisinart Air Fryer Oven work. Once done, serve and enjoy.
Per Serving: Calories 170; Fat 9.4g; Sodium 61mg; Carbs 0.3g; Fiber 0g; Sugar 0.2g; Protein 20.4g

Coconut Cauliflower Tater Tots

Prep time: 15 minutes | Cook time: 10 minutes | Serves: 6

2 pound fresh cauliflower, cut into chunks
1.5 tbsp. Cheddar cheese
1 cup Panko breadcrumbs
1 tsp. desiccated coconut
1 tsp. Oats
1 egg, beaten

2 tbsp. onion, chopped
1 tsp. garlic puree
1 tsp. parsley
1 tsp. chives
1 tsp. oregano
Salt and pepper to taste

1. Fresh cauliflower florets should be cooked for 10 minutes in salted water until tender, and then drained. 2. In a mixing bowl, mash the cauliflower and add salt, black pepper, garlic, parsley, chives, and oregano. Mix thoroughly, then form little tater tots from the mixture. 3. In a tray, combine breadcrumbs, oats, and coconut shreds. 4. After dipping the tater tots in the egg, coat them with the crumb mixture. Arrange the tater tots into the Air Fryer Basket. 5. Place the Air Fryer Basket onto the Baking Pan and insert into rack Position 2. Set the Function Dial to Air Fry. Set Temperature Dial to 360 degrees F, and then turn the ON/Oven Timer dial to 10 minutes. 6. Let the Cuisinart Air Fryer Oven work. Turn the food halfway through. 7. Once done, serve and enjoy.
Per Serving: Calories 140; Fat 5.3g; Sodium 150mg; Carbs 20g; Fiber 6.2g; Sugar 4.5g; Protein 6.2g

Taco-Seasoned Beef Cups

Prep time: 10 minutes | Cook time: 10 minutes | Serves: 4

1 cup cheddar cheese, shredded
2 tablespoons taco seasoning
½ cup tomatoes, chopped

1-pound ground beef, cooked
Wonton wrappers

1. Firmly press the wrappers into the muffin tray. Add ground meat and tomatoes to the top. 2. Season the food with taco seasoning and cheese. Arrange wonton wrappers into the Air Fryer Basket. 3. Place the Air Fryer Basket onto the Baking Pan and insert into rack Position 2. Set the Function Dial to Air Fry. 4. Set Temperature Dial to 350 degrees F, and then turn the ON/Oven Timer dial to 15 minutes. 5. Let the Cuisinart Air Fryer Oven work. Turn the food halfway through. 6. Once done, serve and enjoy.
Per Serving: Calories 537; Fat 26.9g; Sodium 698mg; Carbs 19.2g; Fiber 0.4g; Sugar 0.7g; Protein 52.4g

Honey Veggies

Prep time: 10 minutes | Cook time: 30 minutes | Serves: 4

Vinaigrette
½ cup olive oil
½ cup avocado oil
¼ teaspoon pepper
1 teaspoon salt
Veggies
4 zucchinis, halved
4 sweet onions, quartered
4 red peppers, seeded and halved

2 tablespoons honey
½ cup red wine vinegar
2 tablespoons Dijon Mustard

2 bunch green onions, trimmed
4 yellow squashes, cut in half

1. Whisk together mustard, honey, vinegar, salt, and pepper in a small basin. Mix them with the oil thoroughly. 2. Arrange veggies into the Air Fryer Basket. Place the Air Fryer Basket onto the Baking Pan and insert into rack Position 2. Set the Function Dial to Air Fry. Set Temperature Dial to 350 degrees F, and then turn the ON/Oven Timer dial to 15 minutes. 3. Let the Cuisinart Air Fryer Oven work. Serve with a side of mustard vinaigrette.
Per Serving: Calories 415; Fat 29.3g; Sodium 793mg; Carbs 37g; Fiber 7.6g; Sugar 23.1g; Protein 5.4g

Paprika Chickpeas

Prep time: 05 minutes | Cook time: 10 minutes | Serves: 4

1 (15-oz.) can chickpeas rinsed and dry to out
1 tablespoon olive oil
½ teaspoon ground cumin

½ teaspoon cayenne pepper
½ teaspoon smoked paprika
Salt, as required

1. Add all the ingredients to the Baking Pan and toss them well. Insert the Baking Pan into rack Position 1. Set the Function Dial to Bake. 2. Set Temperature Dial to 390 degrees F, and then turn the ON/Oven Timer dial to 10 minutes. Let the Cuisinart Air Fryer Oven work. 3. Stir the food halfway through. Serve warm.
Per Serving: Calories 159; Fat 4.8g; Sodium 357mg; Carbs 24.4g; Fiber 4.9g; Sugar 0.1g; Protein 5.4 g

Sausage Patties

Prep time: 10 minutes | Cook time: 10 minutes | Serves: 2

1 pack sausage patties

1. Transfer the sausages to into the Baking Pan. Insert the Baking Pan into rack Position 1. Set the Function Dial to Bake. 2. Set Temperature Dial to 400 degrees F, and then turn the ON/Oven Timer dial to 10 minutes. Let the Cuisinart Air Fryer Oven work. 3. Once done, serve and enjoy.
Per Serving: Calories 100; Fat 0.4g; Sodium 350mg; Carbs 5.5g; Fiber 0g; Sugar 0g; Protein 8.4g

Crunchy Peanuts

Prep time: 05 minutes | Cook time: 14 minutes | Serves: 6

1½ cups raw peanuts   Nonstick cooking spray

1. Arrange the peanuts in the Air Fryer Basket, and spray the peanuts with cooking Spray. 2. Place the Air Fryer Basket onto the Baking Pan and insert into rack Position 2. Set the Function Dial to Air Fry. 3. Set Temperature Dial to 320 degrees F, and then turn the ON/Oven Timer dial to 15 minutes. 4. Let the Cuisinart Air Fryer Oven work. Toss the food halfway through. 5. Serve warm.
Per Serving: Calories 207; Fat 18g; Sodium 7mg; Carbs 5.9g; Fiber 3.1g; Sugar 1.5g; Protein 9.4g

Parsley Italian Bread

Prep time: 10 minutes | Cook time: 5 minutes | Serves: 4

Salt to taste   ½ cup butter, melted
1 Italian loaf of bread   4 garlic cloves, chopped
1 tablespoon fresh parsley, chopped

1. Add parsley, butter, and garlic in a bowl. Spread the mixture on the bread slices. 2. Arrange bread slices into the Air Fryer Basket. Place the Air Fryer Basket onto the Baking Pan and insert into rack Position 2. Set the Function Dial to Air Fry. 3. Set Temperature Dial to 400 degrees F, and then turn the ON/Oven Timer dial to 3 minutes. Let the Cuisinart Air Fryer Oven work. 4. Turn the food halfway through. Once done, serve and enjoy.
Per Serving: Calories 236; Fat 23.3g; Sodium 271mg; Carbs 6.6g; Fiber 0.3g; Sugar 0.6g; Protein 1.5g

Creole Almond Tomatoes

Prep time: 10 minutes | Cook time: 5 minutes | Serves: 4

Bread crumbs as needed
½ cup buttermilk
¼ cup almond flour

Salt and pepper to taste
¼ tablespoon Creole seasoning
1 green tomato

1. Take a plate and put flour on it, then take another plate and put buttermilk on it. Season tomatoes with salt and pepper after cutting them up. 2. Combine creole seasoning and breadcrumbs in a bowl. Cover a tomato slice in flour, dip it in buttermilk, and then roll it in crumbs. 3. Make the remaining tomatoes with the same steps. Arrange tomatoes into the Air Fryer Basket. 4. Place the Air Fryer Basket onto the Baking Pan and insert into rack Position 2. Set the Function Dial to Air Fry. 5. Set Temperature Dial to 350 degrees F, and then turn the ON/Oven Timer dial to 5 minutes. 6. Let the Cuisinart Air Fryer Oven work. Turn the food halfway through. When the time is up, carefully remove them from the cooking tray. 7. Once done, serve and enjoy.
Per Serving: Calories 87; Fat 4.3g; Sodium 292mg; Carbs 9.7g; Fiber 1.4g; Sugar 3.4g; Protein 3.8g

Yogurt Blueberry Muffins

Prep time: 10 minutes | Cook time: 10 minutes | Serves: 10

2 teaspoons vanilla extract
1 cup blueberries
½ teaspoon salt
1 cup yogurt
1 to ½ cups cake flour

½ cup sugar
2 teaspoons baking Powder
⅓ cup vegetable oil
1 egg

1. Coat 10 muffin tins in a little coating of cooking oil or spray. Combine the flour, sugar, baking powder, and salt in a medium mixing basin. 2. Combine the yoghurt, oil, egg, and vanilla extract in a medium mixing bowl. Combine the contents of both bowls. Place the chocolate chips on top. 3. Pour the batter evenly into the muffin tins. Arrange muffins into the Air Fryer Basket. 4. Place the Air Fryer Basket onto the Baking Pan and insert into rack Position 2. Set the Function Dial to Air Fry. Set Temperature Dial to 355 degrees F, and then turn the ON/Oven Timer dial to 10 minutes. 5. Let the Cuisinart Air Fryer Oven work. Once done, serve and enjoy.
Per Serving: Calories 204; Fat 8.3g; Sodium 140mg; Carbs 28.7g; Fiber 0.9g; Sugar 13.4g; Protein 4g

Shrimp with Bacon Bites

Prep time: 10 minutes | Cook time: 8 minutes | Serves: 12

½ teaspoon red pepper flakes, crushed
1 tablespoon salt
1 teaspoon chili powder
1¼ pounds shrimp, peeled and deveined
1 teaspoon paprika

½ teaspoon black pepper, ground
1 tablespoon shallot powder
¼ teaspoon cumin powder
1 to ¼ pounds thin bacon slices

1. In a medium to sized mixing dish, thoroughly combine the shrimp and seasoning until evenly coated. 2. Wrap a piece of bacon around each shrimp, attach with a toothpick, and chill for 30 minutes. Arrange shrimps into the Air Fryer Basket. 3. Place the Air Fryer Basket onto the Baking Pan and insert into rack Position 2. Set the Function Dial to Air Fry. 4. Set Temperature Dial to 350 degrees F, and then turn the ON/ Oven Timer dial to 15 minutes. Let the Cuisinart Air Fryer Oven work. Turn the food halfway through. 5. Once done, serve and enjoy.
Per Serving: Calories 314; Fat 20.6g; Sodium 1292mg; Carbs 1.7g; Fiber 0.2g; Sugar 0.1g; Protein 28.8g

Beef Quinoa Meatballs

Prep time: 10 minutes | Cook time: 15 minutes | Serves: 6

1 cup quinoa, cooked
1 beaten egg
½ to pound pork, ground
½ to pound beef, ground
2 scallions, chopped
½ teaspoon onion powder
1 to ½ tablespoons Dijon mustard

1 tablespoon sesame oil
2 tablespoons tamari sauce
¾ cup ketchup
1 teaspoon ancho chili powder
¼ cup balsamic vinegar
2 tablespoons sugar

1. Mix the ingredients completely in a medium to sized mixing basin and form small meatballs from it. Arrange meatballs into the Air Fryer Basket. 2. Place the Air Fryer Basket onto the Baking Pan and insert into rack Position 2. Set the Function Dial to Air Fry. Set Temperature Dial to 370 degrees F, and then turn the ON/Oven Timer dial to 5 minutes. 3. Let the Cuisinart Air Fryer Oven work. Turn the food halfway through. When the time is up, carefully remove them from the cooking tray. 4. Once done, serve and enjoy.
Per Serving: Calories 307; Fat 8g; Sodium 768mg; Carbs 31.7g; Fiber 2.4g; Sugar 11.4g; Protein 27.8g

Sweet Apple Dumplings

Prep time: 10 minutes | Cook time: 15 minutes | Serves: 2

2 tablespoons raisins
2 apples, smallest possible size, peeled and cored
1 tablespoon brown sugar

2 tablespoon butter, melted
2 sheets puff pastry

1. Place the apples in the pastry sheets and fill the cores with the sugar and raisins. Fold the pastries one by one to make dumplings. 2. Using a pastry brush, coat the dumplings in butter. Arrange dumplings into the Baking Pan. Insert the Baking Pan into rack Position 1. Set the Function Dial to Bake. 3. Set Temperature Dial to 350 degrees F, and then turn the ON/Oven Timer dial to 15 minutes. 4. Let the Cuisinart Air Fryer Oven work. Once done, serve and enjoy.
Per Serving: Calories 482; Fat 27g; Sodium 506mg; Carbs 62.7g; Fiber 6.8g; Sugar 34g; Protein 4g

Squash Bites

Prep time: 10 minutes | Cook time: 15 minutes | Serves: 6

1 ½ pounds winter squash, peeled and make chunks
¼ cup dark brown sugar
2 tablespoons sage, chopped
Zest of 1 small to sized lemon

2 tablespoons coconut oil, melted
A coarse pinch salt
A pinch pepper
⅛ teaspoon allspice, ground

1. Except for the squash, thoroughly combine all of the ingredients in a medium to sized mixing bowl. Mixture should completely cover the squash chunks. 2. Arrange squash into the Baking Pan. Insert the Baking Pan into rack Position 1. Set the Function Dial to Bake. 3. Set Temperature Dial to 350 degrees F, and then turn the ON/Oven Timer dial to 15 minutes. Let the Cuisinart Air Fryer Oven work. 4. Once done, serve and enjoy.
Per Serving: Calories 337; Fat 14.3g; Sodium 16mg; Carbs 57g; Fiber 6.4g; Sugar 13.4g; Protein 3.3g

Cayenne Pickle Slices

Prep time: 15 minutes | Cook time: 18 minutes | Serves: 8

16 dill pickle slices
¼ cup all to purpose flour
Salt, as required
2 small eggs, beaten lightly
1 tablespoon dill pickle juice

¼ teaspoon garlic powder
¼ teaspoon cayenne pepper
1 cup panko breadcrumbs
1 tablespoon fresh dill, minced
Cooking Spray

1. Place the pickle slices on paper towels for about 15 minutes or until the liquid has been absorbed completely. 2. Meanwhile, combine the flour and salt in a small dish. In a separate shallow dish, whisk together the eggs, pickle juice, garlic powder, and cayenne. 3. Combine the panko and dill in a third shallow dish. Coat the pickle slices in flour, then dip them in the egg mixture, and finally in the panko mixture. 4. Arrange pickle slices into the Air Fryer Basket. Place the Air Fryer Basket onto the Baking Pan and insert into rack Position 2. Set the Function Dial to Air Fry. 5. Set Temperature Dial to 400 degrees F, and then turn the ON/Oven Timer dial to 18 minutes. Let the Cuisinart Air Fryer Oven work. 6. Turn the food halfway through. Once done, serve and enjoy.
Per Serving: Calories 67; Fat 1.3g; Sodium 476mg; Carbs 11.4g; Fiber 1.4g; Sugar 0.6g; Protein 2.8g

Bacon—Wrapped Poppers

Prep time: 15 minutes | Cook time: 12 minutes | Serves: 4

6 jalapeños (about 4" long each)
3 ounces full to fat cream cheese
⅓ cup shredded medium Cheddar cheese

¼ teaspoon garlic powder
12 slices sugar to free bacon

1. Remove the tops of the jalapenos and cut them down the middle lengthwise into two pieces. Carefully remove the white membrane and seeds from the peppers with a knife. 2. Combine cream cheese, Cheddar, and garlic powder in a large microwave to safe container. Stir after 30 seconds in the microwave. 3. Fill hollow jalapenos with cheese mixture. Wrap a slice of bacon over each jalapeno half, completely wrapping it; season with salt and pepper. 4. Arrange jalapenos into the Air Fryer Basket. Place the Air Fryer Basket onto the Baking Pan and insert into rack Position 2. Set the Function Dial to Air Fry. 5. Set Temperature Dial to 400 degrees F, and then turn the ON/Oven Timer dial to 12 minutes. Let the Cuisinart Air Fryer Oven work. 6. Turn the food halfway through. Once done, serve and enjoy.
Per Serving: Calories 73; Fat 4.1g; Sodium 215mg; Carbs 2.7g; Fiber 0.6g; Sugar 0.9g; Protein 6.2g

Potato Fries

Prep time: 15 minutes | Cook time: 16 minutes | Serves: 2

½ pound potatoes, peeled and cut into ½-inch thick sticks lengthwise

1 tablespoon olive oil
Salt and ground black pepper

1. Combine all of the ingredients in a large mixing bowl and toss well to combine. Arrange potatoes sticks into the Air Fryer Basket. 2. Place the Air Fryer Basket onto the Baking Pan and insert into rack Position 2. Set the Function Dial to Air Fry. 3. Set Temperature Dial to 400 degrees F, and then turn the ON/Oven Timer dial to 16 minutes. Let the Cuisinart Air Fryer Oven work. 4. Turn the food halfway through. Once done, serve and enjoy.
Per Serving: Calories 138; Fat 7.1g; Sodium 7mg; Carbs 17.6g; Fiber 2.7g; Sugar 1.6g; Protein 1.9g

Ham Potato Balls

Prep time: 10 minutes | Cook time: 5 minutes | Serves: 6

½ cup ham, chopped
½ cup Colby cheese, shredded
2 ounces soft cheese
3 cups potatoes, mashed

1 egg; slightly beaten
2 green onions, sliced
1 cup seasoned breadcrumbs
2½ tablespoons canola oil

1. Except for the breadcrumbs and canola oil, thoroughly combine the ingredients in a medium mixing bowl. Make little balls out of it. 2. Arrange balls into the Air Fryer Basket. Place the Air Fryer Basket onto the Baking Pan and insert into rack Position 2. Set the Function Dial to Air Fry. 3. Set Temperature Dial to 350 degrees F, and then turn the ON/Oven Timer dial to 15 minutes. Let the Cuisinart Air Fryer Oven work. Turn the food halfway through. 4. Once done, serve and enjoy.
Per Serving: Calories 249; Fat 13.3g; Sodium 465mg; Carbs 24.7g; Fiber 1.4g; Sugar 3.4g; Protein 3.8g

Vegetable Spring Rolls

Prep time: 10 minutes | Cook time: 13 minutes | Serves: 8

2 cups green cabbage, shredded
2 yellow onions, chopped.
1 carrot, grated
8 spring roll sheets
2 tbsp. corn flour
2 tbsp. water
½ chili pepper, minced

1 tbsp. ginger, grated
3 garlic cloves, minced
1 tsp. sugar
1 tsp. soy sauce
2 tbsp. olive oil
Salt and black pepper to the taste

1. Add the cabbage, onions, carrots, chili pepper, ginger, garlic, sugar, salt, pepper, and soy sauce to a skillet over medium heat with the oil. 2. Stir thoroughly and simmer them for 2 to 3 minutes, then remove from heat and wait for a few minutes to cool. 3. Cut the spring roll sheets into squares, divide the cabbage mixture among them, and roll them up. 4. Combine corn flour and water in a mixing dish, stir well, and use this mixture to seal spring rolls. Arrange rolls into the Air Fryer Basket. 5. Place the Air Fryer Basket onto the Baking Pan and insert into rack Position 2. Set the Function Dial to Air Fry. 6. Set Temperature Dial to 360 degrees F, and then turn the ON/Oven Timer dial to 10 minutes. 7. Let the Cuisinart Air Fryer Oven work. Turn the food halfway through. 8. Once done, serve and enjoy.
Per Serving: Calories 236; Fat 4.7g; Sodium 57mg; Carbs 44.6g; Fiber 2.7g; Sugar 3.6g; Protein 4.8g

Crab Sticks

Prep time: 10 minutes | Cook time: 12 minutes | Serves: 4

2 oz. Crab sticks, halved
2 tsp. Cajun seasoning

2 tsp. sesame oil

1. Toss crab sticks with sesame oil and Cajun seasoning in a bowl. Arrange crab sticks into the Air Fryer Basket. 2. Place the Air Fryer Basket onto the Baking Pan and insert into rack Position 2. Set the Function Dial to Air Fry. 3. Set Temperature Dial to 350 degrees F, and then turn the ON/Oven Timer dial to 12 minutes. Let the Cuisinart Air Fryer Oven work. 4. Turn the food halfway through. Once done, serve and enjoy.
Per Serving: Calories 67; Fat 4.5g; Sodium 50mg; Carbs 3.7g; Fiber 0g; Sugar 0g; Protein 2.6g

Salmon-Potato Patties

Prep time: 15 minutes | Cook time: 22 minutes | Serves: 4

3 big potatoes boiled, drained and mashed
1 egg
1 big salmon fillet, skinless, boneless
2 tbsps. bread crumbs

2 tbsps. parsley, chopped
2 tbsps. dill, chopped
Salt and black pepper to the taste
Cooking Spray

1. Arrange salmon into the Baking Pan. Insert the Baking Pan into rack Position 1. Set the Function Dial to Bake. 2. Set Temperature Dial to 360 degrees F, and then turn the ON/Oven Timer dial to 10 minutes. Let the Cuisinart Air Fryer Oven work. 3. Cool the salmon on a cutting board before flaking it and placing it in a bowl. Stir in the mashed potatoes, salt, pepper, dill, parsley, egg, and bread crumbs, and form 8 patties from the mixture. 4. Arrange salmon patties into the Air Fryer Basket. Place the Air Fryer Basket onto the Baking Pan and insert into rack Position 2. Set the Function Dial to Air Fry. 5. Set Temperature Dial to 350 degrees F, and then turn the ON/Oven Timer dial to 12 minutes. Let the Cuisinart Air Fryer Oven work. Turn the food halfway through. 6. Once done, serve and enjoy.
Per Serving: Calories 254; Fat 4.5g; Sodium 75mg; Carbs 48.6g; Fiber 4.5g; Sugar 2.2g; Protein 14.8g

Spinach Chicken Breast

Prep time: 10 minutes | Cook time: 17 minutes | Serves: 4

4 chicken breasts, boneless and skinless
1 cup sun dried tomatoes, chopped.
2 cups baby spinach
1 to ½ tbsp. Italian seasoning

4 mozzarella slices
A drizzle of olive oil
Salt and black pepper to the taste

1. Using a meat tenderizer, flatten the chicken breasts, divide the tomatoes, mozzarella, and spinach, season with salt, pepper, and Italian seasoning, then roll and seal them. 2. Arrange chicken rolls into the Air Fryer Basket. Place the Air Fryer Basket onto the Baking Pan and insert into rack Position 2. Set the Function Dial to Air Fry. 3. Set Temperature Dial to 375 degrees F, and then turn the ON/Oven Timer dial to 17 minutes. Let the Cuisinart Air Fryer Oven work. 4. Turn the food halfway through. Once done, serve and enjoy.
Per Serving: Calories 449; Fat 23.8g; Sodium 377mg; Carbs 8.3g; Fiber 1.9g; Sugar 0.4g; Protein 50.3g

Cheese Broccoli Tots

Prep time: 10 minutes | Cook time: 15 minutes | Serves: 4

1 to pound broccoli, grated
½ cup cheddar cheese, shredded
1 tablespoon extra to virgin olive oil
1 egg

½ cup panko breadcrumbs
2 cloves garlic, minced
Sea salt and freshly ground black pepper, to taste

1. Combine all of the ingredients thoroughly. Form the mixture into equal to sized balls and arrange them in a single layer in the Air Fryer Basket. 2. Place the Air Fryer Basket onto the Baking Pan and insert into rack Position 2. Set the Function Dial to Air Fry. 3. Set Temperature Dial to 390 degrees F, and then turn the ON/ Oven Timer dial to 10 minutes. Let the Cuisinart Air Fryer Oven work. 4. Turn the food halfway through. Once done, serve and enjoy.
Per Serving: Calories 179; Fat 9.9g; Sodium 209mg; Carbs 15.8g; Fiber 4g; Sugar 2.3g; Protein 9.2g

Basil Pesto Crackers

Prep time: 10 minutes | Cook time: 17 minutes | Serves: 6

½ tsp. baking Powder
¼ tsp. basil, dried
1 to ¼ cups flour
1garlic clove, minced

2 tbsp. basil pesto
3 tbsp. butter
Salt and black pepper to the taste

1. Combine salt, pepper, baking powder, flour, garlic, cayenne, basil, pesto, and butter in a mixing bowl and whisk until a dough forms. 2. Spread the dough into the Air Fryer Basket. Place the Air Fryer Basket onto the Baking Pan and insert into rack Position 2. Set the Function Dial to Air Fry. 3. Set Temperature Dial to 325 degrees F, and then turn the ON/Oven Timer dial to 17 minutes. Let the Cuisinart Air Fryer Oven work. Turn the food halfway through. 4. Allow the dish to cool before cutting into crackers and serving as a snack.
Per Serving: Calories 128; Fat 6g; Sodium 207mg; Carbs 4.6g; Fiber 2g; Sugar 1.6g; Protein 1.8g

Italian Seasoning Mozzarella Sticks

Prep time: 1 hour and 05 minutes | Cook time: 10 minutes | Serves: 4

1 tablespoon Italian seasoning
1 cup parmesan cheese
8 string cheeses, diced

2 eggs, beaten
1 clove garlic, minced

1. In a mixing bowl, combine the parmesan, garlic, and Italian seasoning. Dip your cheese into the egg and thoroughly mix it up. Roll it in your crumbled cheese, then press the crumbs into the cheese. 2. Place them in the fridge for an hour; arrange the mozzarella sticks to the cooking tray of the air fryer. the Air Fryer Basket. 3. Place the Air Fryer Basket onto the Baking Pan and insert into rack Position 2. Set the Function Dial to Air Fry. 4. Set Temperature Dial to 375 degrees F, and then turn the ON/Oven Timer dial to 10 minutes. Let the Cuisinart Air Fryer Oven work. 5. Turn the food halfway through. When the Mozzarella Sticks are cooked, carefully remove them from the cooking tray
Per Serving: Calories 226; Fat 16.7g; Sodium 517mg; Carbs 3g; Fiber 0g; Sugar 0.5g; Protein 21.1 g

Chat Banana Chips

Prep time: 10 minutes | Cook time: 15 minutes | Serves: 4

½ tsp. turmeric powder
½ tsp. chat masala
1 tsp. olive oil

4 bananas, peeled and sliced
A pinch of salt

1. Combine banana slices, salt, turmeric, chat masala, and oil in a mixing basin and let aside for 10 minutes. 2. Arrange banana slices into the AirFryer Basket. Place the Air Fryer Basket onto the Baking Pan and insert into rack Position 2. Set the Function Dial to Air Fry. Set Temperature Dial to 360 degrees F, and then turn the ON/Oven Timer dial to 15 minutes. Let the Cuisinart Air Fryer Oven work. 3. Once done, serve and enjoy.
Per Serving: Calories 116; Fat 1.8g; Sodium 237mg; Carbs 28g; Fiber 3.1g; Sugar 14.6g; Protein 1.4g

Paprika Dill Pickles

Prep time: 15 minutes | Cook time: 12 minutes | Serves: 4

16 oz. jarred dill pickles
½ cup white flour
1 egg
¼ cup ranch sauce

¼ cup milk
½ tsp. garlic powder
½ tsp. sweet paprika
Cooking Spray

1. In a mixing dish, whisk together the milk and the egg. In a separate bowl, whisk together flour, salt, garlic powder, and paprika. 2. Place pickles in the Air Fryer Basket after dipping them in flour, egg mix, then flour again. Grease them with the cooking spray. 3. Place the Air Fryer Basket onto the Baking Pan and insert into rack Position 2. Set the Function Dial to Air Fry. 4. Set Temperature Dial to 400 degrees F, and then turn the ON/Oven Timer dial to 15 minutes. 5. Let the Cuisinart Air Fryer Oven work. Turn the food halfway through. Once done, serve and enjoy.
Per Serving: Calories 105; Fat 2.7g; Sodium 1028mg; Carbs 16.2g; Fiber 1.8g; Sugar 2.6g; Protein 4.3g

Fried Tomatoes

Prep time: 10 minutes | Cook time: 20 minutes | Serves: 2

2 tomatoes, halved
1 tsp. parsley, dried
1 tsp. basil, dried
1 tsp. oregano, dried

1 tsp. rosemary, dried
Cooking; Spray
Salt and black pepper

1. Spray tomato halves with cooking oil, season with salt, pepper, parsley, basil, oregano and rosemary over them. Arrange tomato halves into the Air Fryer Basket. 2. Place the Air Fryer Basket onto the Baking Pan and insert into rack Position 2. Set the Function Dial to Air Fry. 3. Set Temperature Dial to 320 degrees F, and then turn the ON/Oven Timer dial to 20 minutes. Let the Cuisinart Air Fryer Oven work. 4. Turn the food halfway through. Once done, serve and enjoy.
Per Serving: Calories 27; Fat 0.4g; Sodium 7mg; Carbs 5.7g; Fiber 2.1g; Sugar 3.3g; Protein 1.2g

Chapter 3 Fish and Seafood Recipes

Cod with Cherry Tomatoes

Prep time: 15 minutes | Cook time: 15 minutes | Serves: 4

1 cup cherry tomatoes; halved
4 cod fillets, skinless and boneless
2 tablespoons olive oil

2 tablespoons Cilantro; chopped.
Salt
Pepper

1. Mix all the ingredients in the AirFryer Basket. Place the Air Fryer Basket onto the Baking Pan and insert into rack Position 2. Set the Function Dial to Air Fry. Set Temperature Dial to 370 degrees F, and then turn the ON/Oven Timer dial to 15 minutes. Let the Cuisinart Air Fryer Oven work. 2. Divide everything between plates and serve right away.

Per serving: Calories 285; Fat 9.8g; Sodium 639mg; Carbs 11.1g; Fiber 1.2g, Sugars 5.1g; Protein 27.8g

Crab Dip

Prep time: 15 minutes | Cook time: 8 minutes | Serves: 4

8 oz. full to fat cream cheese; softened.
2 (6 to oz.) can lump crabmeat
¼ cup chopped pickled jalapeños.
¼ cup full to fat sour cream.
½ cup shredded cheddar cheese

¼ cup full to fat mayo
1 tablespoon lemon juice
¼ cup sliced green onion
½ teaspoon hot sauce

1. Place all ingredients into the Baking Pan and toss until thoroughly combined. 2. Insert the Baking Pan into rack Position 1. Set the Function Dial to Bake. Set Temperature Dial to 400 degrees F, and then turn the ON/Oven Timer dial to 8 minutes. 3. Let the Cuisinart Air Fryer Oven work. When done, the dip will be bubbling and hot,

Per serving: Calories 336; Fat 17.3g; Sodium 281mg; Carbs 8.1g; Fiber 5.3g, Sugars 17.7g; Protein 32.3g

Crispy Fillets

Prep time: 15 minutes | Cook time: 15 minutes | Serves: 2

2 fish fillets halved
1egg, beaten
½ cup seasoned breadcrumbs
1 tablespoon balsamic vinegar

½ teaspoon seasoned salt
1 teaspoon paprika
½ teaspoon ground black pepper
1 teaspoon celery seed

1. In a bowl, add the breadcrumbs, vinegar, pepper, salt, paprika, and celery seeds and mix well. 2. Coat the fish fillets with the beaten egg; then, coat them with the breadcrumbs mixture. 3. Pour them into the Baking Pan. Insert the Baking Pan into rack Position 1. Set the Function Dial to Bake. Set Temperature Dial to 350 degrees F, and then turn the ON/Oven Timer dial to 15 minutes. 4. Let the Cuisinart Air Fryer Oven work. Serve.

Per serving: Calories 344; Fat 14.9g; Sodium 227mg; Carbs 14g; Fiber 1g; Sugars 1.4g; Protein 25.7g

Maple Salmon

Prep time: 15 minutes | Cook time: 12 minutes | Serves: 4

4 salmon fillets
2 tablespoons olive oil
¼ cups Dijon mustard

¼ cups maple syrup
2 garlic cloves, minced
Salt and black pepper, to taste

1. Place salmon fillets into the Air Fryer Basket. Stir Dijon mustard, maple syrup, garlic, olive oil, pepper, salt, and pour over salmon. Coat well and let the food sit for 10 minutes. 2. Place the Air Fryer Basket onto the Baking Pan and insert into rack Position 2. Set the Function Dial to Air Fry. Set Temperature Dial to 400 degrees F, and then turn the ON/Oven Timer dial to 12 minutes. 3. Let the Cuisinart Air Fryer Oven work. Turn the food halfway through. Serve.
Per serving: Calories 236; Fat 13.9g; Sodium 451mg; Carbs 13.2g; Fiber 1.2g; Sugars 1.4g; Protein 14.3g

Spiced Tilapia

Prep time: 15 minutes | Cook time: 15 minutes | Serves: 2

1 to pound tilapia fillets
1 tablespoon garlic, minced
2 tablespoon dried parsley

1 tablespoon olive oil
Salt and black pepper, to taste

1. Place the tilapia fillets on the Air Fryer Basket. Drizzle with oil and season with salt and black pepper. 2. Sprinkle parsley and garlic over fish fillets. Place the Air Fryer Basket onto the Baking Pan and insert into rack Position 2. Set the Function Dial to Air Fry. 3. Set Temperature Dial to 400 degrees F, and then turn the ON/Oven Timer dial to 15 minutes. Let the Cuisinart Air Fryer Oven work. 4. Turn the food halfway through. Serve warm.
Per serving: Calories 285; Fat 9.8g; Sodium 639mg; Carbs 11.1g; Fiber 1.2g, Sugars 5.1g; Protein 27.8g

Lime Shrimp

Prep time: 15 minutes | Cook time: 15 minutes | Serves: 4

1 to pound shrimp, peel and deveined
3 garlic cloves, pressed
2 tablespoons lime juice

2 tablespoons butter, melted
¼ cups fresh cilantro, chopped

1. Add shrimp into the Air Fryer Basket. Stir together lime juice, garlic, and butter and pour over shrimp. 2. Place the Air Fryer Basket onto the Baking Pan and insert into rack Position 2. Set the Function Dial to Air Fry. 3. Set Temperature Dial to 375 degrees F, and then turn the ON/Oven Timer dial to 15 minutes. Let the Cuisinart Air Fryer Oven work. 4. Turn the food halfway through. Garnish the dish with cilantro and serve warm.
Per serving: Calories 249; Fat 13g; Sodium 556mg; Carbs 10g; Sugar 1.1g; Fiber 0.7g; Protein 31g

Garlic Tilapia Fillets

Prep time: 15 minutes | Cook time: 20 minutes | Serves: 4

4 tilapia fillets; boneless
1 bunch kale; chopped.
3 garlic cloves; minced
1 teaspoon Fennel seeds

½ teaspoon red pepper flakes, crushed
3 tablespoons olive oil
Salt and black pepper, to taste

1. Coat the fillets with the remaining ingredients and place in the Air Fryer Basket. 2. Place the Air Fryer Basket onto the Baking Pan and insert into rack Position 2. Set the Function Dial to Air Fry. 3. Set Temperature Dial to 360 degrees F, and then turn the ON/Oven Timer dial to 20 minutes. 4. Let the Cuisinart Air Fryer Oven work. Serve.
Per serving: Calories 285; Fat 9.8g; Sodium 639mg; Carbs 11.1g; Fiber 1.2g, Sugars 5.1g; Protein 27.8g

Beer–Battered Cod

Prep time: 15 minutes | Cook time: 15 minutes | Serves: 4

2 eggs
1 cup malty beer
½ cup cornstarch
1 teaspoon garlic powder

1 cup all to purpose flour
Salt and black pepper, to taste
4 (4-ounce / 113-g) cod fillets

1. In a bowl, beat together the 2 eggs with the beer. In another bowl, thoroughly combine the flour and cornstarch. 2. Sprinkle with the garlic powder, pepper and salt. Dredge cod fillet in the flour mixture, then in the 1 egg mixture. Dip piece of fish in the flour mixture a second time. 3. Arrange the cod fillets in the AirFryer Basket. Place the Air Fryer Basket onto the Baking Pan and insert into rack Position 2. Set the Function Dial to Air Fry. 4. Set Temperature Dial to 400 degrees F, and then turn the ON/Oven Timer dial to 15 minutes. Let the Cuisinart Air Fryer Oven work. 5. Serve.
Per serving: Calories 361; Fat 10g; Sodium 218mg; Carbs 16g; Sugar 1.2g; Fiber 0.7g; Protein 24g

Greek Salmon

Prep time: 15 minutes | Cook time: 25 minutes | Serves: 4

4 salmon fillets
½ cup pesto
1 onion, chopped

2 cups grape tomatoes, halved
½ cup feta cheese, crumbled

1. Line the cooking tray with foil and set aside. Place salmon fillet in the Air Fryer Basket and top with tomatoes, pesto, onion, and cheese. 2. Place the Air Fryer Basket onto the Baking Pan and insert into rack Position 2. Set the Function Dial to Air Fry. 3. Set Temperature Dial to 350 degrees F, and then turn the ON/ Oven Timer dial to 25 minutes. Let the Cuisinart Air Fryer Oven work. 4. Serve.
Per serving: Calories 236; Fat 13.9g; Sodium 451mg; Carbs 13.2g; Fiber 1.2g; Sugars 1.4g; Protein 14.3g

Tilapia and Chips

Prep time: 15 minutes | Cook time: 15 minutes | Serves: 4

1 egg

Old Bay seasoning

½ cup panko breadcrumbs

2 tablespoons almond flour

4 to 6-ounce tilapia fillets

Frozen crinkle cut fries

1. Add almond flour to a bowl, beat 1 egg in another bowl, and add panko breadcrumbs to the third bowl, mixed with Old Bay seasoning. 2. Dredge tilapia fillets in flour, then egg, and then breadcrumbs. Place the coated tilapia fillets in the Air Fryer Basket along with fries. 3. Place the Air Fryer Basket onto the Baking Pan and insert into rack Position 2. Set the Function Dial to Air Fry. 4. Set Temperature Dial to 350 degrees F, and then turn the ON/Oven Timer dial to 15 minutes. Let the Cuisinart Air Fryer Oven work. 5. Serve.

Per serving: Calories 285; Fat 9.8g; Sodium 639mg; Carbs 11.1g; Fiber 1.2g, Sugars 5.1g; Protein 27.8g

Mustard–Crusted Fillets

Prep time: 15 minutes | Cook time: 10 minutes | Serves: 4

5 teaspoon low to sodium yellow mustard

1 tablespoon lemon juice

4 (3.5-ounce / 99-g) sole fillets

⅛ teaspoon freshly ground pepper

1 slice low to sodium whole to wheat bread, crumbled

1 teaspoon olive oil

½ teaspoon dried marjoram

½ teaspoon dried thyme

1. Whisk together the mustard and lemon juice in a bowl until thoroughly mixed and smooth. Spread the mixture evenly over the sole fillets, and then transfer the fillets to the Air Fryer Basket. 2. In a separate bowl, combine the olive oil, thyme, marjoram, pepper, and bread crumbs and stir to mix well. 3. Gently but firmly press the mixture over fillets, coating them completely. 4. Place the Air Fryer Basket onto the Baking Pan and insert into rack Position 2. Set the Function Dial to Air Fry. 5. Set Temperature Dial to 320 degrees F, and then turn the ON/Oven Timer dial to 10 minutes. Let the Cuisinart Air Fryer Oven work. 6. Serve warm.

Per serving: Calories 327; Fat 15g; Sodium 548mg; Carbs 12g; Sugar 1.2g; Fiber 0.7g; Protein 29g

Crusted Salmon Patties

Prep time: 15 minutes | Cook time: 13 minutes | Serves: 2

1 pound (454 g) salmon, chopped into ½-inch pieces

2 tablespoon coconut flour

2 tablespoon grated Parmesan cheese

½ tablespoon milk

½ white onion, peeled and finely chopped

½ teaspoon butter, at room temperature

½ teaspoon chipotle powder

½ teaspoon dried parsley flakes

1 teaspoon acceptable salt

⅓ teaspoon ground black pepper

⅓ teaspoon smoked cayenne pepper

1. Put all the ingredients for the salmon patties in a bowl and stir to combine well. 2. Scoop out 2 tablespoons of the salmon mixture and shape into a patty with your palm, about ½ inches thick. 3. Repeat until all the combination is used. Transfer to the refrigerator for about 120 minutes until firm. 4. When ready, arrange the salmon patties in the Air Fryer Basket. Place the Air Fryer Basket onto the Baking Pan and insert into rack Position 2. Set the Function Dial to Air Fry. 5. Set Temperature Dial to 395 degrees F, and then turn the ON/Oven Timer dial to 13 minutes. 6. Let the Cuisinart Air Fryer Oven work. Serve.

Per serving: Calories 361; Fat 10g; Sodium 218mg; Carbs 16g; Sugar 1.2g; Fiber 0.7g; Protein 24g

Walnut Salmon

Prep time: 15 minutes | Cook time: 15 minutes | Serves: 4

4 salmon fillets
¼ cups walnuts
¼ cups parmesan cheese, grated

1 tablespoon lemon rind
1 teaspoon olive oil

1. Line the cooking tray with foil and set aside. Place salmon fillets in the Air Fryer Basket. Add walnuts into the blender and blend until ground. 2. Mix together walnuts, cheese, oil, and lemon rind and spread on top of salmon fillets. 3. Place the Air Fryer Basket onto the Baking Pan and insert into rack Position 2. Set the Function Dial to Air Fry. 4. Set Temperature Dial to 400 degrees F, and then turn the ON/Oven Timer dial to 15 minutes. Let the Cuisinart Air Fryer Oven work. 5. Serve.

Per serving: Calories 351; Fat 22g; Sodium 502mg; Carbs 15.2g; Sugar 1.1g; Fiber 0.7g; Protein 26.4g

Crusted Halibut Fillets

Prep time: 15 minutes | Cook time: 10 minutes | Serves: 2

2 medium halibut fillets
Dash of Tabasco sauce
½ teaspoon hot paprika
1 teaspoon curry powder
½ teaspoon ground coriander

Kosher salt and freshly cracked mixed peppercorns
2 eggs
1½ tablespoon olive oil
½ cup grated parmesan cheese

1. On a clean work surface, drizzle the halibut fillets with the Tabasco sauce. 2. Sprinkle them with the curry powder, hot paprika, coriander, salt, and cracked mixed peppercorns. Set aside. 3. In a bowl, beat the 2 eggs until frothy. In another bowl, combine the oil and Parmesan cheese. 4. 1 at a time, dredge the fillets in the beaten 2 eggs, shaking off any excess, then roll them over the Parmesan cheese until evenly coated. 5. Arrange the halibut fillets in the Air Fryer Basket in a single layer. Place the Air Fryer Basket onto the Baking Pan and insert into rack Position 2. Set the Function Dial to Air Fry. 6. Set Temperature Dial to 365 degrees F, and then turn the ON/Oven Timer dial to 10 minutes. Let the Cuisinart Air Fryer Oven work. 7. Serve.

Per serving: Calories 254; Fat 28g; Sodium 346mg; Carbs 12.3g; Sugar 1g; Fiber 0.7g; Protein 24.3 g

Parmesan Cod Fillets

Prep time: 15 minutes | Cook time: 20 minutes | Serves: 4

4 cod fillets; boneless
A drizzle of olive oil
3 spring onions; chopped.

1 cup parmesan
4 tablespoons balsamic vinegar
Salt and black pepper, to taste

1. Season the cod fillets with pepper, salt, grease with the oil, and coat it in parmesan. Put the fillets in the Air Fryer Basket. 2. Place the Air Fryer Basket onto the Baking Pan and insert into rack Position 2. Set the Function Dial to Air Fry. 3. Set Temperature Dial to 370 degrees F, and then turn the ON/Oven Timer dial to 20 minutes. Let the Cuisinart Air Fryer Oven work. 4. In a bowl, toss the spring onions with salt, pepper, the vinegar and whisk well. Divide the cod between plates, drizzle the spring onions mix all over and serve with a side salad. 5. Serve.

Per serving: Calories 344; Fat 14.9g; Sodium 227mg; Carbs 14g; Fiber 1g; Sugars 1.4g; Protein 25.7g

Artichoke Paella

Prep time: 15 minutes | Cook time: 9 minutes | Serves: 4

1 (10-ounce) package frozen cooked rice, thawed
6-ounce jar artichoke hearts, drained and chopped
½ teaspoon turmeric
½ teaspoon dried thyme

¼ cup vegetable broth
1 cup frozen cooked small shrimp
½ cup frozen baby peas
1 tomato, diced

1. Combine the rice, artichoke hearts, vegetable broth, turmeric, and thyme in the Baking Pan, and stir gently. 2. Insert the Baking Pan into rack Position 1. Set the Function Dial to Bake. Set Temperature Dial to 350 degrees F, and then turn the ON/Oven Timer dial to 9 minutes. 3. Let the Cuisinart Air Fryer Oven work. When done, gently stir in the shrimp, peas, and tomato. 4. Serve.
Per serving: Calories 236; Fat 13.9g; Sodium 451mg; Carbs 13.2g; Fiber 1.2g; Sugars 1.4g; Protein 14.3g

Salmon with Cauliflower

Prep time: 15 minutes | Cook time: 15 minutes | Serves: 4

4 salmon fillets; boneless
½ cup chicken stock
1 cup cauliflower, riced

1 teaspoon turmeric powder
Salt and black pepper, to taste
1 tablespoon butter; melted

1. In the Baking Pan, mixes the cauliflower rice with the other ingredients except the salmon, and toss Arrange the salmon fillets over the cauliflower rice. 2. Insert the Baking Pan into rack Position 1. Set the Function Dial to Bake. Set Temperature Dial to 360 degrees F, and then turn the ON/Oven Timer dial to 15 minutes. 3. Let the Cuisinart Air Fryer Oven work. Serve.
Per serving: Calories 285; Fat 9.8g; Sodium 639mg; Carbs 11.1g; Fiber 1.2g, Sugars 5.1g; Protein 27.8g

Salmon with Coconut Sauce

Prep time: 15 minutes | Cook time: 25 minutes | Serves: 4

4 salmon fillets; boneless
½ cup coconut; shredded
¼ cup coconut cream
⅓ cup heavy cream

¼ cup lime juice
1 teaspoon lime zest; grated
A pinch of Salt and black pepper, to taste

1. Mix all the ingredients except the salmon in a bowl. Arrange the fish in the Air Fryer Basket on the Baking Pan, drizzle the coconut sauce all over. 2. Insert them in rack Position 2. Set the Function Dial to Air Fry. Set Temperature Dial to 360 degrees F, and then turn the ON/Oven Timer dial to 25 minutes. 3. Let the Cuisinart Air Fryer Oven work. Serve.
Per serving: Calories 305; Fat 15g; Sodium 548mg; Carbs 12g; Sugar 1.2g; Fiber 0.7g; Protein 29g

Salmon and Sauce

Prep time: 15 minutes | Cook time: 25 minutes | Serves: 2

4 salmon fillets; boneless
2 garlic cloves; minced
1 tablespoon Chives; chopped.
1 teaspoon lemon juice

¼ cup ghee; melted
½ cup heavy cream
1 teaspoon Dill; chopped.
A pinch of salt and black pepper

1. Mix all the ingredients except the salmon in a bowl. Arrange the salmon in the Air Fryer Basket on the Baking Pan, drizzle the sauce all over. 2. Insert them in rack Position 2. Set the Function Dial to Air Fry. Set Temperature Dial to 360 degrees F, and then turn the ON/Oven Timer dial to 25 minutes. 3. Let the Cuisinart Air Fryer Oven work. Serve.
Per serving: Calories 344; Fat 14.9g; Sodium 227mg; Carbs 14g; Fiber 1g; Sugars 1.4g; Protein 25.7g

Dill Salmon Patties

Prep time: 15 minutes | Cook time: 10 minutes | Serves: 2

1 egg
1 teaspoon dill weeds
½ cup almond flour

14 oz. salmon
¼ cups onion, diced

1. Add all ingredients to the bowl and stir well. Make patties from bowl mixture and place into the Air Fryer Basket. 2. Place the Air Fryer Basket onto the Baking Pan and insert into rack Position 2. Set the Function Dial to Air Fry. Set Temperature Dial to 375 degrees F, and then turn the ON/Oven Timer dial to 10 minutes. 3. Let the Cuisinart Air Fryer Oven work. Serve.
Per serving: Calories 285; Fat 9.8g; Sodium 639mg; Carbs 11.1g; Fiber 1.2g, Sugars 5.1g; Protein 27.8g

Salmon Patties

Prep time: 15 minutes | Cook time: 7 minutes | Serves: 2

1 egg, lightly beaten
8 oz. salmon fillet, minced
Salt and black pepper, to taste

¼ teaspoon garlic powder
¼ teaspoon onion powder

1. Add all ingredients into the bowl and stir until just combined. Make small patties from the salmon mixture and place into the Air Fryer Basket. 2. Place the Air Fryer Basket onto the Baking Pan and insert into rack Position 2. Set the Function Dial to Air Fry. 3. Set Temperature Dial to 400 degrees F, and then turn the ON/ Oven Timer dial to 7 minutes. Let the Cuisinart Air Fryer Oven work. 4. Serve warm.
Per serving: Calories 249; Fat 13g; Sodium 556mg; Carbs 10g; Sugar 1.1g; Fiber 0.7g; Protein 31g

Shrimp with Sesame Seeds

Prep time: 15 minutes | Cook time: 12 minutes | Serves: 4

1 to pound shrimp; peeled and deveined
1 tablespoon olive oil
1 tablespoon sesame seeds, toasted

½ teaspoon Italian seasoning
A pinch of Salt and black pepper, to taste

1. Mix the shrimp with the rest of the ingredients in a bowl. Put the shrimp in the Air Fryer Basket. 2. Place the Air Fryer Basket onto the Baking Pan and insert into rack Position 2. Set the Function Dial to Air Fry. 3. Set Temperature Dial to 370 degrees F, and then turn the ON/Oven Timer dial to 12 minutes. Let the Cuisinart Air Fryer Oven work. 4. Serve.
Per serving: Calories 344; Fat 14.9g; Sodium 227mg; Carbs 14g; Fiber 1g; Sugars 1.4g; Protein 25.7g

Cauliflower Sole Fritters

Prep time: 15 minutes | Cook time: 28 minutes | Serves: 2

½ pound (227 g) sole fillets
½ pound (227 g) mashed cauliflower
½ cup red onion, chopped
1 egg, beaten
3 garlic cloves, minced
Cooking spray
2 tablespoons fresh parsley, chopped

1 tablespoon olive oil
1 tablespoon coconut amino
½ teaspoon scotch bonnet pepper, minced
½ teaspoon paprika
1 bell pepper, finely chopped
Salt and white pepper

1. Place the sole fillets in the Air Fryer Basket. Place the Air Fryer Basket onto the Baking Pan and insert into rack Position 2. Set the Function Dial to Air Fry. 2. Set Temperature Dial to 380 degrees F, and then turn the ON/Oven Timer dial to 14 minutes. Let the Cuisinart Air Fryer Oven work. 3. When cooking is complete, transfer the fish fillets to a bowl. Mash the fillets into flakes. 4. Add the remaining ingredients and toss to combine. Scoop out 2 tablespoons of the fish mixture and shape into a patty about ½ inches thick with your hands. 5. Repeat with the remaining fish mixture. Place the cakes in the cooking tray and return to the Baking Pan. Bake them in the Cuisinart Air Fryer Oven at 380 degrees F for 14 minutes more. 6. When done, serve warm.
Per serving: Calories 361; Fat 10g; Sodium 218mg; Carbs 16g; Sugar 1.2g; Fiber 0.7g; Protein 24g

Flavorful Shrimp

Prep time: 15 minutes | Cook time: 6 minutes | Serves: 2

½ pound shrimp, peeled and deveined
½ teaspoon old bay seasoning
½ teaspoon cayenne pepper

¼ teaspoon paprika
1 tablespoon extra to virgin olive oil
Pinch of salt

1. Add shrimp and remaining ingredients into the bowl and mix well to coat. Add shrimp into the Air Fryer Basket. 2. Place the Air Fryer Basket onto the Baking Pan and insert into rack Position 2. Set the Function Dial to Air Fry. 3. Set Temperature Dial to 400 degrees F, and then turn the ON/Oven Timer dial to 6 minutes. Let the Cuisinart Air Fryer Oven work. 4. Serve.
Per serving: Calories 285; Fat 9.8g; Sodium 639mg; Carbs 11.1g; Fiber 1.2g, Sugars 5.1g; Protein 27.8g

Spicy Tilapia Fillets

Prep time: 15 minutes | Cook time: 15 minutes | Serves: 4

4 tilapia fillets
½ teaspoon red chili powder
1 tablespoon fresh lemon juice
3 teaspoons fresh parsley, chopped

1 teaspoon garlic, minced
3 tablespoon butter, melted
1 lemon, sliced
Salt and black pepper, to taste

1. Place fish fillets in the Air Fryer Basket and season with pepper and salt. 2. Mix together butter, garlic, red chili powder, and lemon juice and pour over fish fillets. Arrange lemon slices on top of fish fillets. 3. Place the Air Fryer Basket onto the Baking Pan and insert into rack Position 2. Set the Function Dial to Air Fry. 4. Set Temperature Dial to 350 degrees F, and then turn the ON/Oven Timer dial to 15 minutes. Let the Cuisinart Air Fryer Oven work. 5. Garnish the dish with parsley. Serve.

Per serving: Calories 305; Fat 15g; Sodium 548mg; Carbs 12g; Sugar 1.2g; Fiber 0.7g; Protein 29g

Sticky Tuna

Prep time: 15 minutes | Cook time: 5 minutes | Serves: 4

½ cup hoisin sauce
2 tablespoon rice wine vinegar
1 teaspoon garlic powder
1 cup cooked jasmine rice
¼ teaspoon red pepper flakes

½ small onion, quartered and thinly sliced
8 ounces (227 g) fresh tuna, cut into 1-inch cubes
Cooking spray
2 teaspoon sesame oil
2 teaspoon dried lemongrass

1. In a bowl, mix together the hoisin sauce, sesame oil, vinegar, lemongrass, garlic powder, and red pepper flakes. 2. Add the sliced onion and tuna cubes and gently toss until the fish is evenly coated. Arrange the coated tuna cubes in the sprayed the Air Fryer Basket. 3. Place the Air Fryer Basket onto the Baking Pan and insert into rack Position 2. Set the Function Dial to Air Fry. 4. Set Temperature Dial to 350 degrees F, and then turn the ON/Oven Timer dial to 5 minutes. Let the Cuisinart Air Fryer Oven work. 5. Serve the dish with the cooked jasmine rice.

Per serving: Calories 344; Fat 14.9g; Sodium 227mg; Carbs 14g; Fiber 1g; Sugars 1.4g; Protein 25.7g

Onion Shrimp Fajitas

Prep time: 15 minutes | Cook time: 15 minutes | Serves: 4

1 to pound shrimp, peeled and deveined
1 medium onion, sliced
½ lime juice

½ tablespoon taco seasoning
1 bell pepper, sliced
½ tablespoon extra to virgin olive oil

1. In a bowl, mix shrimp with remaining ingredients. Place shrimp mixture in the Air Fryer Basket. 2. Place the Air Fryer Basket onto the Baking Pan and insert into rack Position 2. Set the Function Dial to Air Fry. 3. Set Temperature Dial to 400 degrees F, and then turn the ON/Oven Timer dial to 15 minutes. Let the Cuisinart Air Fryer Oven work. 4. Serve.

Per serving: Calories 285; Fat 9.8g; Sodium 639mg; Carbs 11.1g; Fiber 1.2g, Sugars 5.1g; Protein 27.8g

Tilapia with Salsa

Prep time: 15 minutes | Cook time: 15 minutes | Serves: 4

4 tilapia fillets; boneless
2 tablespoons Sweet red pepper; chopped.
1 tablespoon balsamic vinegar
12 oz. Canned tomatoes; chopped.

2 tablespoons Green onions; chopped.
1 tablespoon olive oil
A pinch of salt and black pepper

1. Arrange the tilapia in the Air Fryer Basket and season with salt and pepper. 2. In a bowl, combine all the other ingredients, stir and spread over the fish. 3. Place the Air Fryer Basket onto the Baking Pan and insert into rack Position 2. Set the Function Dial to Air Fry. Set Temperature Dial to 350 degrees F, and then turn the ON/Oven Timer dial to 15 minutes. 4. Let the Cuisinart Air Fryer Oven work. Serve.
Per serving: Calories 254; Fat 28g; Sodium 346mg; Carbs 12.3g; Sugar 1g; Fiber 0.7g; Protein 24.3 g

Tilapia with Gold Potatoes

Prep time: 15 minutes | Cook time: 20 minutes | Serves: 4

10 ounces Yukon Gold potatoes, sliced ¼-inch thick
1 tablespoon unsalted butter, melted, divided
1 teaspoon kosher salt, divided
4 (8-ounce) tilapia fillets

½ pound green beans, trimmed
2 tablespoons chopped fresh parsley, for garnish
Juice of 1 lemon

1. Drizzle the potatoes with 2 tablespoons of melted butter and ¼ teaspoon of kosher salt in a bowl. Transfer the potatoes to the Air Fryer Basket. 2. Place the Air Fryer Basket onto the Baking Pan and insert into rack Position 2. Set the Function Dial to Air Fry. 3. Set Temperature Dial to 375 degrees F, and then turn the ON/Oven Timer dial to 20 minutes. Let the Cuisinart Air Fryer Oven work. 4. Meanwhile, season both sides of the fillets with ½ teaspoon of kosher salt. Put the green beans in a bowl and sprinkle with the remaining ¼ teaspoon of kosher salt and 1 tablespoon of butter, tossing to coat. 5. After 10 minutes, remove the tray and push the potatoes to 1 side. Put the fillets in the middle of the tray and add the green beans on the other side. 6. Drizzle the rest of the 2 tablespoons of butter over the fillets. Return the food to the air fryer oven and cook until the fish flakes easily with a fork, and the green beans are crisp to tender. 7. Once cooked, remove and drizzle the lemon juice over the fillets and sprinkle the parsley on top for garnish. 8. Serve.
Per serving: Calories 361; Fat 10g; Sodium 218mg; Carbs 16g; Sugar 1.2g; Fiber 0.7g; Protein 24g

Trout with Pine Nuts

Prep time: 15 minutes | Cook time: 16 minutes | Serves: 4

1 avocado, peeled, pitted, and roughly chopped.
4 rainbow trout
⅓ pine nuts
3 garlic cloves; minced
½ cup mint; chopped.

1 cup + 3 tablespoons olive oil
1 cup parsley; chopped
Zest of 1 lemon
Juice of 1 lemon
A pinch of Salt and black pepper, to taste

1. Pat dry the trout, season with salt and pepper, and rub with 3 tablespoons of oil. Put the fish in the Air Fryer Basket. 2. Place the Air Fryer Basket onto the Baking Pan and insert into rack Position 2. Set the Function Dial to Air Fry. 3. Set Temperature Dial to 350 degrees F, and then turn the ON/Oven Timer dial to 16 minutes. Let the Cuisinart Air Fryer Oven work. 4. Divide the fish between plates and drizzle half of the lemon juice all over. 5. In a blender, combine the rest of the oil with the remaining lemon juice, parsley, garlic, mint, pine nuts, lemon zest, and the avocado and pulse well. Spread this over the trout. 6. Serve.
Per serving: Calories 236; Fat 13.9g; Sodium 451mg; Carbs 13.2g; Fiber 1.2g; Sugars 1.4g; Protein 14.3g

Lemon Bacon Shrimps

Prep time: 15 minutes | Cook time: 10 minutes | Serves: 6

1 package bacon
1 to pound shrimp
½ teaspoon cayenne pepper
½ teaspoon ground cumin
½ teaspoon onion powder

1 teaspoon garlic powder
½ teaspoon lemon zest
1 tablespoon lemon juice
1 tablespoon Worcestershire sauce

1. In a mixing bowl, whisk the Worcestershire sauce, cumin, lemon zest, lemon juice, cayenne pepper, onion powder, and garlic powder. 2. Add and combine the shrimp. Refrigerate for 1 to 2 hours to marinate. 3. Take the bacon, slice into 2 parts, and wrap the shrimp with them. Add the wrapped shrimps to the Air Fryer Basket. 4. Place the Air Fryer Basket onto the Baking Pan and insert into rack Position 2. Set the Function Dial to Air Fry. 5. Set Temperature Dial to 380 degrees F, and then turn the ON/Oven Timer dial to 10 minutes. Let the Cuisinart Air Fryer Oven work. 6. Serve

Per serving: Calories 351; Fat 22g; Sodium 502mg; Carbs 15.2g; Sugar 1.1g; Fiber 0.7g; Protein 26.4g

Cajun Salmon

Prep time: 15 minutes | Cook time: 8 minutes | Serves: 2

2 salmon fillets (6 ounces and with skin)
1 tablespoon Cajun seasoning

1 teaspoon brown Sugar
Cooking oil spray

1. In a mixing bowl, combine the Cajun seasoning and brown sugar. Add the fillets and coat well. 2. Spray the Air Fryer Basket with some cooking oil, and add the fillets. 3. Place the Air Fryer Basket onto the Baking Pan and insert into rack Position 2. Set the Function Dial to Air Fry. 4. Set Temperature Dial to 350 degrees F, and then turn the ON/Oven Timer dial to 8 minutes. 5. Let the Cuisinart Air Fryer Oven work. When the display indicates "turn Food", flip the fillets, and continue cooking for the remaining time. 6. Serve.

Per serving: Calories 344; Fat 14.9g; Sodium 227mg; Carbs 12g; Fiber 1.2g; Sugars 1g; Protein 27g

Coconut Shrimp

Prep time: 15 minutes | Cook time: 12 minutes | Serves: 6

3 cups panko breadcrumbs
½ cup all to purpose flour
2 eggs
¼ cup honey
2 teaspoons fresh cilantro, chopped
3 cups flaked coconut, unsweetened
12-ounce medium to size raw shrimps, peeled, and

deveined
1 Serrano chili, thinly sliced
¼ cup lime juice
½ teaspoon kosher salt
½ teaspoon ground black pepper
Cooking spray

1. In a mixing bowl, combine the honey, Serrano chili with lime juice. In the second bowl, combine the salt, pepper and flour. 2. In the third bowl, beat the 2 eggs. In the fourth bowl, combine the coconut and breadcrumbs. 3. Coat the shrimps with the eggs first, then with the flour, and then with the crumbs. Coat the shrimps with some cooking spray. 4. Line the Air Fryer Basket with a parchment paper, add the shrimps. Place the Air Fryer Basket onto the Baking Pan and insert into rack Position 2. Set the Function Dial to Air Fry. 5. Set Temperature Dial to 350 degrees F, and then turn the ON/Oven Timer dial to 12 minutes. Let the Cuisinart Air Fryer Oven work. 6. Toss the food halfway through. Serve the shrimps warm with the chili sauce.

Per serving: Calories 305; Fat 15g; Sodium 548mg; Carbs 12g; Sugar 1.2g; Fiber 0.7g; Protein 29g

Creamed Cod Fillets

Prep time: 15 minutes | Cook time: 14 minutes | Serves: 2

1 tablespoon lemon juice
1 to pound cod fillets
2 tablespoons olive oil
Sauce:
3 tablespoon ground mustard
½ cup heavy cream

½ teaspoon ground black pepper
½ teaspoon salt

1 tablespoon butter
½ teaspoon salt

1. Spread some olive oil on the fillets. Season the fillets with the pepper, salt, and lemon juice. 2. Grease the AirFryer Basket with some cooking spray. Place the fillets over it. 3. Place the Air Fryer Basket onto the Baking Pan and insert into rack Position 2. Set the Function Dial to Air Fry. 4. Set Temperature Dial to 400 degrees F, and then turn the ON/Oven Timer dial to 10 minutes. Let the Cuisinart Air Fryer Oven work. 5. In a bowl, add the heavy cream, mustard sauce, heavy cream, and salt. Cook the sauce for 3 to 4 minutes in a saucepan over medium heat. 6. Pour it over the fish and serve warm.
Per serving: Calories 285; Fat 9.8g; Sodium 639mg; Carbs 11.1g; Fiber 1.2g, Sugars 5.1g; Protein 27.8g

Lemon Shrimp

Prep time: 15 minutes | Cook time: 6 minutes | Serves: 4

¼ teaspoon, crushed red pepper flakes
4 cloves garlic, finely grated
1 tablespoon olive oil
1 pound small shrimps, peeled and deveined

Lemon juice, zested
¼ cup, parsley, chopped
¼ teaspoon salt

1. Remove the tails of the shrimps. In a mixing bowl, add shrimps, the garlic, lemon zest, red pepper flakes, salt, and oil. 2. Combine the ingredients to stir well with other. In the Air Fryer Basket, add the shrimps. 3. Place the Air Fryer Basket onto the Baking Pan and insert into rack Position 2. Set the Function Dial to Air Fry. 4. Set Temperature Dial to 400 degrees F, and then turn the ON/Oven Timer dial to 6 minutes. Let the Cuisinart Air Fryer Oven work. 5. Serve warm with the lemon juice and parsley on top.
Per serving: Calories 344; Fat 14.9g; Sodium 227mg; Carbs 14g; Fiber 1g; Sugars 1.4g; Protein 25.7g

Chapter 4 Vegetable and Sides Recipes

Fried Leeks

Prep time: 5 minutes | Cook time: 10 minutes | Serves: 4

4 leeks; ends cut off and halved
1 tablespoon butter; melted

1 tablespoon lemon juice
Salt and black pepper to the taste

1. Coat the leeks in melted butter, season with salt & pepper. 2. Cook for 7 minutes at 400 degrees F on Air Fry mode in the Cuisinart Air Fryer Oven. 3. Arrange on a plate and sprinkle with lemon juice before serving.
Per Serving: Calories 100; Fat 4g; Sodium 338mg; Carbs 6g; Fiber 2g; Sugar 2g; Protein 2g

Parmesan Radishes

Prep time: 5 minutes | Cook time: 15 minutes | Serves: 4

½ teaspoon onion powder
⅓ cup parmesan; grated
4 eggs

1 pound radishes; sliced
Salt and black pepper to the taste

1. Combine radishes, salt, pepper, onion, eggs, and parmesan in a mixing bowl and toss well. Cook the radishes for 7 minutes at 400 degrees F on Air Fry mode in Cuisinart Air Fryer Oven. 2. Serve the hash on individual plates.
Per Serving: Calories 80; Fat 5g; Sodium 449mg; Carbs 5g; Fiber 2g; Sugar 2g; Protein 7g

Cheese Broccoli

Prep time: 20 minutes | Cook time: 15 minutes | Serves: 4

12 ounces frozen broccoli, thawed, drained, and patted dry
1 large egg, lightly beaten
½ cup seasoned whole to wheat bread crumbs
¼ cup shredded reduced to fat sharp Cheddar cheese

¼ cup grated Parmesan cheese
1½ teaspoons minced garlic
Salt and freshly ground black pepper, to taste
Cooking spray

1. Grease the AirFryer Basket with cooking spray. 2. In a food processor, combine the other ingredients and pulse until the mixture resembles coarse meal. 3. Place the ingredients in a mixing basin. Scoop out the broccoli mixture with a tablespoon and shape into 24 oval "tater tot" shapes with your hands. 4. Place the tots in a single layer in the pan, spacing them 1 inch apart. Using a thin mist of cooking spray, gently coat the tots. 5. Place the AirFryer Basket onto the Baking Pan and insert into rack Position 2. Set the Function Dial to Air Fry. 6. Set Temperature Dial to 400 degrees F, and then turn the ON/Oven Timer dial to 15 minutes. Let the Cuisinart Air Fryer Oven work. 7. Turn the food halfway through. When done, the tots will be lightly browned and crispy. 8. Remove from the air fryer oven and serve on a plate.
Per Serving: Calories 211; Fat 12 g; Sodium 443mg; Carbs 14 g; Fiber 2g; Sugar 4g; Protein 8 g

Spicy Broccoli Florets

Prep time: 5 minutes | Cook time: 15 minutes | Serves: 4

1-pound broccoli florets
1 tablespoon olive oil
1 tablespoons chili sauce

Juice of 1 lime
A pinch of salt and black pepper

1. In a large mixing basin, combine all of the ingredients and toss thoroughly. 2. Place the broccoli in the Air Fryer Basket. Cook the food for 15 minutes at 400 degrees F on Air Fry mode in the Cuisinart Air Fryer Oven. 3. Serve by dividing the mixture amongst plates.
Per Serving: Calories 173 g; Fat 6 g; Sodium 299mg; Carbs 6 g; Fiber 2 g; Sugar 1g; Protein 8 g

Asparagus and Broccoli

Prep time: 5 minutes | Cook time: 15 minutes | Serves: 4

1 broccoli head, florets separated
½ pound asparagus, trimmed
Juice of 1 lime

Salt and black pepper to the taste
2 tablespoons olive oil
3 tablespoons parmesan, grated

1. Stir the asparagus with the broccoli and all of the other ingredients, except the parmesan, in a small bowl, toss, put to your Air Fryer Basket. 2. Cook them for 15 minutes at 400 degrees F on Air Fry mode in the Cuisinart Air Fryer Oven. 3. Serve by dividing the pasta amongst plates and sprinkling the parmesan on top.
Per Serving: Calories 172; Fat 5 g; Sodium 399mg; Carbs 4 g; Fiber 2 g; Sugar 1g; Protein 9g

Broccoli Mix

Prep time: 5 minutes | Cook time: 15 minutes | Serves: 4

1-pound broccoli florets
A pinch of salt and black pepper

1 teaspoon sweet paprika
½ tablespoon butter, melted

1. Toss the broccoli with the other ingredients in a small mixing dish. Place the broccoli in the Air Fryer Basket. 2. Cook for 15 minutes at 350 degrees F on Air Fry mode in the Cuisinart Air Fryer Oven, then divide into plates and serve.
Per Serving: Calories 130; Fat 3 g; Sodium 267mg; Carbs 4 g; Fiber 3 g; Sugar 1g; Protein 8 g

Broccoli Salad

Prep time: 5 minutes | Cook time: 20 minutes | Serves: 4

1 broccoli head; florets separated
1 tablespoon Chinese rice wine vinegar
1 tablespoon peanut oil

6 garlic cloves; minced
Salt and black pepper to the taste

1. Toss broccoli with salt, pepper, and half of the oil in a bowl, then put to your air fryer. 2. Cook the food for 8 minutes at 400 degrees F on Air Fry mode in the Cuisinart Air Fryer Oven, tossing the food halfway through. 3. Transfer broccoli to a salad dish, mix with the remaining peanut oil, garlic, and rice vinegar, and serve.
Per Serving: Calories 121; Fat 3 g; Sodium 383mg; Carbs 4 g; Fiber 4 g; Sugar 2g; Protein 4 g

Kale with Balsamic

Prep time: 2 minutes | Cook time: 12 minutes | Serves: 6

2 tablespoons olive oil
3 garlic cloves, minced
2 and ½ pounds kale leaves

Salt and black pepper to the taste
2 tablespoons balsamic vinegar

1. Toss all of the ingredients together in the Air Fryer Basket on the Baking Pan. 2. Cook for 12 minutes at 400 degrees F on Air Fry mode in the Cuisinart Air Fryer Oven. 3. Serve by dividing the mixture amongst plates.

Per Serving: Calories 122; Fat 4 g; Sodium 336mg; Carbs 4 g; Fiber 3 g; Sugar 2g; Protein 5 g

Olives with Kale

Prep time: 5 minutes | Cook time: 15 minutes | Serves: 4

½ pounds kale, torn
1 tablespoon olive oil
Salt and black pepper to the taste

1 tablespoon hot paprika
1 tablespoon black olive, pitted and sliced

1. Toss all of the ingredients together in the Air Fryer Basket on the Baking Pan. 2. Place the pan in your air fryer and cook for 15 minutes at 400 degrees F on Air Fry mode in the Cuisinart Air Fryer Oven. 3. Divide into plates and serve.

Per Serving: Calories 154 g; Fat 3 g; Sodium 298mg; Carbs 4 g; Fiber 2 g; Sugar 2g; Protein 6 g

Crunchy Masala Broccoli

Prep time: 10 minutes | Cook time: 8 minutes | Serves: 2

¼ teaspoon masala
½ teaspoon red chili powder
½ teaspoon salt
¼ teaspoon turmeric powder

1 tablespoon chickpea flour
1 tablespoon yogurt
1-pound broccoli

1. Cut the broccoli into florets. To eliminate impurities, soak for at least half an hour in a bowl of water with 2 tablespoons of salt. 2. Remove the broccoli florets from the water and set them aside to drain. Wipe off the surface completely. 3. To make a marinade, combine all of the other ingredients. In a large mixing bowl, toss the broccoli florets with the marinade. Chill for 15 to 30 minutes, covered. 4. Place the marinated broccoli florets in the Air Fryer Basket. Place the Air Fryer Basket onto the Baking Pan and insert into rack Position 2. 5. Set the Function Dial to Air Fry. Set Temperature Dial to 400 degrees F, and then turn the ON/Oven Timer dial to 10 minutes. Let the Cuisinart Air Fryer Oven work. 6. When the Florets are done, they will be crispy.

Per Serving: Calories 96; Fat 1.3g; Sodium 241mg; Carbs 3g; Fiber 2g; Sugar 1g; Protein 7g

Kale with Oregano

Prep time: 5 minutes | Cook time: 10 minutes | Serves: 4

1-pound kale, torn
1 tablespoon olive oil

A pinch of salt and black pepper
2 tablespoons oregano, chopped

1. Toss all of the ingredients together in the Baking Pan. 2. Cook the food for 10 minutes at 380 degrees F on Bake mode in the Cuisinart Air Fryer Oven. 3. Serve by dividing the mixture amongst plates.
Per Serving: Calories 140; Fat 3 g; Sodium 220mg; Carbs 3 g; Fiber 2 g; Sugar 0g; Protein 5 g

Brussels Sprout & Kale

Prep time: 5 minutes | Cook time: 15 minutes | Serves: 8

1 pound Brussels sprouts, trimmed
1 cups kale, torn
1 tablespoon olive oil

Salt and black pepper to the taste
3 ounces mozzarella, shredded

1. Toss all of the ingredients except the mozzarella in the Baking Pan. 2. Cook for 15 minutes at 380 degrees F on Bake mode in the Cuisinart Air Fryer Oven. 3. Serve by dividing the mixture across plates and sprinkling the cheese on top.
Per Serving: Calories 170; Fat 5 g; Sodium 449mg; Carbs 4 g; Fiber 3 g; Sugar 0g; Protein 7 g

Avocado Olives Mix

Prep time: 5 minutes | Cook time: 15 minutes | Serves: 4

2 cups kalamata olives, pitted
2 small avocados, pitted, peeled, and sliced
¼ cup cherry tomatoes, halved

Juice of 1 lime
1 tablespoon coconut oil, melted

1. Combine the olives with the other ingredients in the Air Fryer Basket on the Baking Pan, stir them well. 2. Cook the food at 400 degrees F for 15 minutes on Air Fry mode in the Cuisinart Air Fryer Oven. 3. Serve the mixture by dividing it amongst plates.
Per Serving: Calories 153; Fat 3 g; Sodium 331mg; Carbs 4 g; Fiber 3 g; Sugar 1g; Protein 6 g

Mushrooms with Kale

Prep time: 5 minutes | Cook time: 15 minutes | Serves: 4

1-pound brown mushrooms, sliced
1-pound kale, torn
Salt and black pepper to the taste

2 tablespoons olive oil
14 ounces coconut milk

1. Toss the kale with the rest of the ingredients in the Baking Pan. 2. Place the pan in the air fryer and cook for 15 minutes at 400 degrees F on Bake mode in the Cuisinart Air Fryer Oven. 3. Divide into plates and serve.
Per Serving: Calories 162; Fat 4 g; Sodium 331mg; Carbs 3 g; Fiber 1 g; Sugar 0g; Protein 5 g

Bacon with Green Beans

Prep time: 5 minutes | Cook time: 15 minutes | Serves: 4

½ pound green beans, trimmed and halved
1 cup black olives, pitted and halved
¼ cup bacon, cooked and crumbled

1 tablespoon olive oil
¼ cup tomato sauce

1. Combine all of the ingredients in the Baking Pan. 2. Cook for 15 minutes at 380 degrees F on Bake mode in the Cuisinart Air Fryer Oven. 3. Serve the dish by dividing the mixture amongst plates.
Per Serving: Calories 160; Fat 4 g; Sodium 270mg; Carbs 5 g; Fiber 3 g; Sugar 1g; Protein 4 g

Cajun Peppers

Prep time: 4 minutes | Cook time: 12 minutes | Serves: 4

1 tablespoon olive oil
½ pound mixed bell peppers, sliced

1 cup black olives, pitted and halved
½ tablespoon Cajun seasoning

1. Combine all of the ingredients in the Baking Pan. Cook the food for 12 minutes at 400 degrees F on Bake mode in the Cuisinart Air Fryer Oven. 2. Serve the mixture by dividing it amongst plates.
Per Serving: Calories 151; Fat 3 g; Sodium 226mg; Carbs 4 g; Fiber 2 g; Sugar 2g; Protein 5 g

Butter Tomatoes

Prep time: 5 minutes | Cook time: 8 minutes | Serves: 4

1 tablespoon of herbed butter
4 large tomatoes

1 cup of mozzarella cheese, shredded

1. Set the air fryer to Roast for 10 minutes at 380 degrees F. 2. Scoop out the tomato's interior contents and stuff it with cheese. Toss the filled tomatoes with the herbed butter and place on the Baking Pan. 3. Bake the food at 380 degrees F for 10 minutes in the Cuisinart Air Fryer Oven. 4. Warm the dish before serving.
Per Serving: Calories 75; Fat 3.2g; Sodium 310mg; Carbs 7.5g; Fiber 2g; Sugar 2g; Protein 5g

Simple Asparagus

Prep time: 10 minutes | Cook time: 9 minutes | Serves: 4

1 to pound asparagus, cut the ends
1 teaspoon olive oil

Pepper
Salt

1. Arrange asparagus on the Baking Pan. Season the food with pepper and salt and drizzle with olive oil. 2. Bake asparagus at 365 degrees F for 7 to 9 minutes in the Cuisinart Air Fryer Oven. 3. Turn the food halfway through. Serve and have fun.
Per Serving: Calories 33; Fat 1.3 g; Sodium 312mg; Carbs 4.4 g; Fiber 1g; Sugar 2.1 g; Protein 2.5 g

Spicy and Herby Eggplants

Prep time: 15 minutes | Cook time: 15 minutes | Serves: 2

½ teaspoon dried marjoram, crushed
½ teaspoon dried oregano, crushed
½ teaspoon dried thyme, crushed
½ teaspoon garlic powder

Salt and ground black pepper, as required
1 large eggplant, cubed
Olive oil cooking spray

1. Combine herbs, garlic powder, salt, and black pepper in a small bowl. 2. After uniformly spraying the eggplant cubes with cooking spray, combine them with the herb mixture. 3. Arrange eggplant cubes in a single layer in the Air Fryer Basket. Place the Air Fryer Basket onto the Baking Pan and insert into rack Position 2. Set the Function Dial to Air Fry. 4. Set Temperature Dial to 400 degrees F, and then turn the ON/ Oven Timer dial to 15 minutes. Let the Cuisinart Air Fryer Oven work. 5. Flip the eggplant cubes and spray them with cooking spray after 6 minutes of cooking time. 6. When done, serve warm.
Per Serving: Calories 62; Fat 0.5g; Sodium 310mg; Carbs 14.5g; Fiber 7g; Sugar 3g; Protein 2.4g

Veggies with Basil

Prep time: 15 minutes | Cook time: 20 minutes | Serves: 2

1 small eggplant, halved and sliced
1 yellow bell pepper, sliced into 1 inch strips
1 red bell pepper, sliced into 1 inch strips
1 garlic clove, quartered
1 red onion, sliced

1 tablespoon extra to virgin olive oil
Salt and freshly ground black pepper, to taste
½ cup chopped fresh basil, for garnish
Cooking spray

1. Grease the Baking Pan with cooking spray. 2. Combine the eggplant, bell peppers, garlic, and red onion in the pan. Drizzle the olive oil over the top and toss to evenly coat. 3. Using cooking spray, saturate all exposed surfaces. Insert the Baking Pan into rack Position 1. Set the Function Dial to Bake. 4. Set Temperature Dial to 365 degrees F, and then turn the ON/Oven Timer dial to 20 minutes. Let the Cuisinart Air Fryer Oven work. 5. Flip the veggies halfway through. Remove the dish from the air fryer oven and season with salt and pepper. 6. Serve with a sprinkling of basil on top as a finishing touch.
Per Serving: Calories 164; Fat 4.1 g; Sodium 222mg; Carbs 6 g; Fiber 2g; Sugar 4g; Protein 7 g

Celery Roots

Prep time: 10 minutes | Cook time: 20 minutes | Serves: 4

2 celery roots, peeled and diced
1 teaspoon extra to virgin olive oil
1 teaspoon butter, melted

½ teaspoon ground cinnamon
Sea salt and freshly ground black pepper, to taste

1. In a large mixing basin, toss the celery roots with the olive oil until completely coated. 2. Place them on the Baking Pan. Insert the Baking Pan into rack Position 1. Set the Function Dial to Bake. 3. Set Temperature Dial to 365 degrees F, and then turn the ON/Oven Timer dial to 20 minutes. Let the Cuisinart Air Fryer Oven work. 4. Celery roots should be quite sensitive when done. Remove the dish from the air fryer oven and place it in a serving bowl. 5. Add the butter and cinnamon and mash until frothy with a potato masher. Season the dish with salt and pepper. 6. Serve right away.
Per Serving: Calories 134; Fat 3 g; Sodium 170mg; Carbs 7 g; Fiber 1g; Sugar 3g; Protein 9 g

Carrot, Zucchini and Squash Mix

Prep time: 5 minutes | Cook time: 35 minutes | Serves: 4

1 tablespoon chopped tarragon leaves
½ teaspoon white pepper
1 teaspoon salt
1-pound yellow squash

1-pound zucchini
6 teaspoons olive oil
½ pound carrots

1. Squash and zucchini should be stemmed and rooted before being cut into ¾-inch half to moons. Carrots should be peeled and sliced into 1-inch pieces. 2. Toss carrot chunks with 2 tablespoons olive oil until well coated. Air-Fry the carrots in the Cuisinart Air Fryer Oven at 400 degrees F for 5 minutes. 3. While the carrots are cooking, pour the remaining olive oil over the squash and zucchini, seasoning with pepper and salt. 4. Toss well to coat. When the timer for the carrots goes off, add the squash and zucchini. 5. Cook them for 30 minutes, tossing 2 to 3 times during the cooking time. 6. 1Remove the vegetables and mix with tarragon after they're done. Warm it up before serving.
Per Serving: Calories 122; Fat 9g; Sodium 441mg; Carbs 7g; Fiber 2g; Sugar 1g; Protein 6g

Basil Tomatoes

Prep time: 10 minutes | Cook time: 10 minutes | Serves: 2

3 tomatoes, halved
Olive oil cooking spray

Salt and ground black pepper
1 tablespoon fresh basil, chopped

1. Spritz cooking spray on the cut sides of the tomato halves equally. Add salt, black pepper, and basil to taste. 2. Add the food to the Air Fryer Basket. Place the Air Fryer Basket onto the Baking Pan and insert into rack Position 2. Set the Function Dial to Air Fry. 3. Set Temperature Dial to 400 degrees F, and then turn the ON/Oven Timer dial to 10 minutes. Let the Cuisinart Air Fryer Oven work. 4. When the device beeps to indicate that it has warmed. Place the tomatoes in an Air Fryer Basket and cook them. 5. Serve warm.
Per Serving: Calories 34; Fat 0.4 g; Sodium 225mg; Carbs 7.2 g; Fiber 2g; Sugar 2g; Protein 1.7 g

Honey Brussels Sprout

Prep time: 10 minutes | Cook time: 15 minutes | Serves: 4

½ pound Brussels sprouts, cut stems then cut each in half
For sauce:
1 tablespoon sriracha sauce
1 tablespoon vinegar
1 tablespoon lemon juice
1 teaspoon sugar

1 tablespoon olive oil
½ tsp. salt

1 tablespoon honey
1 teaspoon garlic, minced
½ teaspoon olive oil

1. In a small saucepan, combine all sauce ingredients and cook over low heat for 2 to 3 minutes or until thickened. Take the saucepan from the heat and set it aside. 2. In a zip to lock bag, combine the Brussels sprouts, oil, and salt and shake thoroughly. Place Brussels sprouts on the Air Fryer Basket. 3. Place the Air Fryer Basket onto the Baking Pan and insert into rack Position 2. Set the Function Dial to Air Fry. 4. Set Temperature Dial to 400 degrees F, and then turn the ON/Oven Timer dial to 15 minutes. Let the Cuisinart Air Fryer Oven work. 5. Toss and fill a mixing dish halfway with Brussels sprouts halfway through. Toss the dish with the prepared sauce until fully coated. 6. Serve and have fun.
Per Serving: Calories 86; Fat 4.3 g; Sodium 223mg; Carbs 11.8 g; Fiber 2g; Sugar 7.6 g; Protein 2 g

Delicious Tomatoes & Broccoli

Prep time: 15 minutes | Cook time: 15 minutes | Serves: 2

2 large tomatoes
½ cup broccoli, chopped finely
½ cup Cheddar cheese, shredded

Salt and ground black pepper
1 tablespoon unsalted butter, melted
½ teaspoon dried thyme, crushed

1. Cut the tops off each tomato carefully and scoop out the pulp and seeds. 2. Chop the broccoli and combine it with the cheese, salt, and black pepper in a mixing bowl. Fill each tomato equally with the broccoli mixture and arrange them in the AirFryer Basket. Place the Air Fryer Basket onto the Baking Pan and insert into rack Position 2. 3. Set the Function Dial to Air Fry. Set Temperature Dial to 400 degrees F, and then turn the ON/Oven Timer dial to 15 minutes. 4. Let the Cuisinart Air Fryer Oven work. Serve warm with the garnishing of thyme.
Per Serving: Calories 206; Fat 15.6 g; Sodium 229mg; Carbs 9 g; Fiber 2g; Sugar 2g; Protein 9.4 g

Cheese Green Beans

Prep time: 10 minutes | Cook time: 5 minutes | Serves: 6

2 pounds fresh green beans
½ cup flour
2 eggs, lightly beaten

¾ tablespoon garlic powder
½ cup parmesan cheese, grated
1 cup breadcrumbs

1. Add flour to a small dish. Add the eggs to a second shallow dish. 2. Combine breadcrumbs, garlic powder, and cheese in a third shallow dish. Coat the beans in flour, then in eggs, and finally in breadcrumbs. 3. Place coated beans on the Air Fryer Basket. Place the Air Fryer Basket onto the Baking Pan and insert into rack Position 2. Set the Function Dial to Air Fry. 4. Set Temperature Dial to 400 degrees F, and then turn the ON/Oven Timer dial to 5 minutes. Let the Cuisinart Air Fryer Oven work. 5. Serve and have fun.
Per Serving: Calories 257; Fat 8.6 g; Sodium 429mg; Carbs 27.2 g; Fiber 4g; Sugar 2.6 g; Protein 14.9 g

Spiced Carrots

Prep time: 10 minutes | Cook time: 20 minutes | Serves: 6

2 pounds carrots, peeled, slice in half again slice half
2 ½ tablespoons dried parsley
1 teaspoon dried oregano
1 teaspoon dried thyme

3 tablespoons olive oil
Pepper
Salt

1. In a mixing basin, combine the carrots. Toss in the remaining ingredients on top of the carrots. 2. Arrange carrots on the Air Fryer Basket. Place the Air Fryer Basket onto the Baking Pan and insert into rack Position 2. Set the Function Dial to Air Fry. 3. Set Temperature Dial to 400 degrees F, and then turn the ON/Oven Timer dial to 20 minutes. Let the Cuisinart Air Fryer Oven work. 4. Turn the food halfway through. Serve and have fun.
Per Serving: Calories 124; Fat 7.1 g; Sodium 410mg; Carbs 15.3 g; Fiber 5.5g; Sugar 7.5 g; Protein 1.3 g

Veggies Mix

Prep time: 10 minutes | Cook time: 18 minutes | Serves: 4

1 cup carrots, sliced
1 cup cauliflower, cut into florets
1 cup broccoli florets

1 tablespoon olive oil
Pepper
Salt

1. Combine all of the veggies in the Baking Pan. Season them with pepper and salt and then drizzle with olive oil. Toss them thoroughly. 2. Insert the Baking Pan into rack Position 1. Set the Function Dial to Bake. Set Temperature Dial to 380 degrees F, and then turn the ON/Oven Timer dial to 18 minutes. 3. Let the Cuisinart Air Fryer Oven work. Serve and have fun.
Per Serving: Calories 55; Fat 3.6 g; Sodium 331mg; Carbs 5.6 g; Fiber 1g; Sugar 2.3 g; Protein 1.4 g

Butter Sweet Potatoes

Prep time: 10 minutes | Cook time: 40 minutes | Serves: 4

4 sweet potatoes, scrubbed and washed
½ tablespoon butter, melted

½ teaspoon sea salt

1. Prick the sweet potatoes. Sweet potatoes should be rubbed with melted butter and seasoned with salt. 2. Select Bake option. Cook sweet potatoes for 40 minutes at 365 degrees F on the Baking Pan. 3. Serve and have fun.
Per Serving: Calories 125; Fat 1.5 g; Sodium 410mg; Carbs 26.2 g; Fiber 7g; Sugar 5.4 g; Protein 2.1 g

Curry Zucchini

Prep time: 5 minutes | Cook time: 8 to 10 minutes | Serves: 2

2 zucchinis, washed & sliced
1 tablespoon olive oil

1 pinch sea salt
Curry mix, pre to made

1. Combine the zucchini slices, salt, oil, and spices in the Air Fryer Basket. 2. Place the Air Fryer Basket onto the Baking Pan and insert into rack Position 2. Set the Function Dial to Air Fry. 3. Set Temperature Dial to 400 degrees F, and then turn the ON/Oven Timer dial to 10 minutes. Let the Cuisinart Air Fryer Oven work. 4. Serve alone or with sour cream.
Per Serving: Calories 100; Fat 1g; Sodium 170mg; Carbs 4g; Fiber 2g; Sugar 1g; Protein 2g

Coconut Cauliflower Pudding

Prep time: 10 minutes | Cook time: 30 minutes | Serves: 4

2½ cups water
1 cup coconut sugar
2 cups cauliflower rice

2 cinnamon sticks
½ cup coconut, shredded

1. Mix water with coconut sugar in the baking pan; add the cauliflower rice, cinnamon, and coconut, whisk, then place in the Cuisinart Air Fryer Oven and cook for 30 minutes at 365 degrees F on Bake mode. 2. Serve the pudding cold, divided into cups. Enjoy!
Per Serving: Calories 203; Fat 4 g; Sodium 331mg; Carbs 9 g; Fiber 1g; Sugar 2g; Protein 4 g

Chapter 5 Poultry Recipes

Chimichurri Chicken Breasts

Prep time: 5 minutes | Cook time: 35 minutes | Serves: 1

1 chicken breast, bone to in, skin to on
Chimichurri
½ bunch fresh cilantro
¼ bunch fresh parsley
½ shallot, peeled, cut in quarters
½ tablespoon paprika ground
½ tablespoon chili powder
½ tablespoon fennel ground
½ teaspoon black pepper, ground

½ teaspoon onion powder
1 teaspoon salt
½ teaspoon garlic powder
½ teaspoon cumin ground
½ tablespoon canola oil
2 tablespoons olive oil
4 garlic cloves, peeled
1 zest and juice of lemon
1 teaspoon kosher salt

1. In a suitable bowl, combine all the spices and season the chicken. Drizzle the chicken with canola oil and place it in the Air Fryer Basket. 2. Place the Air Fryer Basket onto the Baking Pan and insert into rack Position 2. Set the Function Dial to Air Fry. 3. Set Temperature Dial to 400 degrees F, and then turn the ON/Oven Timer dial to 35 minutes. Let the Cuisinart Air Fryer Oven work. 4. In a blender, combine all other ingredients and mix until smooth. Toss the chicken with the Chimichurri sauce and serve.
Per serving: Calories 140; Fat 7.9g; Sodium 581mg; Carbs 1.8g; Fiber 0.1g; Sugar 7.1g; Protein 7.2g

Mayo Chicken Wings

Prep time: 5 minutes | Cook time: 10 minutes | Serves: 8

For Wings
1 teaspoon pepper
1 teaspoon salt
For Sauce
2 packets Splenda
1 tablespoon minced garlic
1 tablespoon minced ginger
1 tablespoon sesame oil
For Finishing
¼ cup chopped green onions

2 pounds of chicken wings

1 teaspoon agave nectar
1 tablespoon mayo
2 tablespoons gochujang

2 teaspoons sesame seeds

1. Season the wings with salt and pepper. 2. Place the wings on the Air Fryer Basket. Place the Air Fryer Basket onto the Baking Pan and insert into rack Position 2. Set the Function Dial to Air Fry. 3. Set Temperature Dial to 400 degrees F, and then turn the ON/Oven Timer dial to 20 minutes. Let the Cuisinart Air Fryer Oven work. 4. Flip the wings halfway through. Combine the sauce ingredients in a mixing bowl as the chicken air fries. 5. Remove the wings and set them in a basin once the chicken has reached 160 degrees F on a thermometer. 6. Pour half of the sauce mixture over the wings and toss to coat thoroughly. Return the painted wings to the Cuisinart Air Fryer Oven for another 5 minutes or until they reach 165 degrees F. 7. Remove the green onions and sesame seeds from the tray. Extra sauce can be dipped in.
Per serving: Calories 356; Fat 26g; Sodium 440mg; Carbs 9g; Fiber 0.5g; Sugar 2g; Protein 23g

Southern-Style Chicken Thighs

Prep time: 15 minutes plus 1 hour for marinating | Cook time: 26 minutes | Serves: 4

½ cup buttermilk
2 teaspoons salt plus 1 tablespoon
1 teaspoon freshly ground black pepper
1 pound chicken thighs (or drumsticks)

1 cup all to purpose flour
2 teaspoons onion powder
2 teaspoons garlic powder
½ teaspoon sweet paprika

1. Whisk together the buttermilk, 2 teaspoons of salt, and pepper in a large mixing basin. Cover the chicken pieces in the basin and marinate for at least an hour in the refrigerator. 2. Prepare the dredging mixture about 5 minutes before the chicken is done marinating. Combine the flour, 1 tablespoon of salt, onion powder, garlic powder, and paprika in a large mixing basin. 3. Olive oil should be sprayed on the cooking tray. Dredge the chicken in the flour mixture after removing it from the buttermilk mixture. 4. Remove any extra flour by shaking it. Place the chicken pieces in a single layer in the Air Fryer Basket, allowing space between each piece. 5. Using a spray bottle, liberally coat the chicken with olive oil. Place the Air Fryer Basket onto the Baking Pan and insert into rack Position 2. Set the Function Dial to Air Fry. 6. Set Temperature Dial to 390 degrees F, and then turn the ON/Oven Timer dial to 26 minutes. Let the Cuisinart Air Fryer Oven work. 7. Flip the chicken thighs halfway through. Check that the chicken has achieved a temperature of 165 degrees F on the inside. 8. If necessary, increase the cooking time. Plate, serve, and enjoy the chicken after it's thoroughly cooked!

Per serving: Calories 377; Fat 18g; Sodium 1182mg; Carbs 28g; Fiber 1g; Sugar 2g; Protein 25g

Cornish Game Hens

Prep time: 10 minutes plus 30 minutes to marinate | Cook time: 20 minutes | Serves: 4

For the Harissa
½ cup olive oil
6 cloves garlic, minced
2 tablespoons smoked paprika
1 tablespoon ground coriander
For the Hens
½ cup yogurt
Cornish game hens, any giblets removed, split in half

1 tablespoon ground cumin
1 teaspoon ground caraway
1 teaspoon kosher salt
½ to 1 teaspoon cayenne pepper

lengthwise

1. Mix the oil, garlic, paprika, coriander, cumin, caraway, salt, and cayenne in a medium microwave to safe bowl to make the harissa. 2. Microwave the harissa for 1 minute on high, stirring halfway during cooking time. Combine 1 to 2 tablespoons of harissa and the yogurt in a small bowl for the chickens. 3. Whisk all of these together until it gets a smooth texture. Pour this mixture and the hen halves in a resealable plastic bag. 4. Seal the bag and massage all the pieces until they are completely covered with a mixture of harissa and yogurt. 5. Then let it marinate at room temperature for 30 minutes or in the refrigerator for up to 24 hours. 6. Arrange the hen halves in the Air Fryer Basket in a single layer. Place the Air Fryer Basket onto the Baking Pan and insert into rack Position 2. Set the Function Dial to Air Fry. 7. Set Temperature Dial to 400 degrees F, and then turn the ON/Oven Timer dial to 20 minutes. Let the Cuisinart Air Fryer Oven work. 8. Serve warm.

Per serving: Calories 590; Fat 38g; Sodium 490mg; Carbs 3.2g; Fiber 0.1g; Sugar 0.1g; Protein 32.5g

Stuffed Chicken Breast

Prep time: 5 minutes | Cook time: 30 minutes | Serves: 2

½ cup Cottage cheese
2 eggs, beaten
2 medium chicken breasts, halved
2 tablespoons fresh coriander, chopped 1 teaspoon

fine sea salt
Seasoned breadcrumbs
⅓ teaspoon freshly ground black pepper, to savor 3
cloves garlic, finely minced

1. Use a meat tenderizer to flatten the chicken breast. 2. Combine the cottage cheese, garlic, coriander, salt, and black pepper in a medium mixing bowl. ⅓ of the mixture should be spread over the first chicken breast. 3. Repeat with the rest of the ingredients. Roll the chicken around the filling, securing it with toothpicks as needed. In a small dish, whisk the egg. 4. Combine the salt, ground black pepper, and seasoned breadcrumbs in a small dish. Roll the chicken breasts in the breadcrumbs after coating them with the whisked egg. 5. Transfer the food to the Air Fryer Basket. Place the Air Fryer Basket onto the Baking Pan and insert into rack Position 2. Set the Function Dial to Air Fry. 6. Set Temperature Dial to 400 degrees F, and then turn the ON/Oven Timer dial to 22 minutes. Let the Cuisinart Air Fryer Oven work. 7. Serve right away.
Per serving: Calories 424; Fat 24.5g; Sodium 580mg; Carbs 7.5g; Fiber 1g; Sugar 1.4g; Protein 43.4g

Aioli Chicken Strips

Prep time: 5 minutes | Cook time: 12 minutes | Serves: 4

3 chicken breasts cut into strips
2 tablespoons olive oil
1 cup breadcrumbs
Salt and black pepper to taste

½ tablespoon garlic powder
½ cup mayonnaise
1 tablespoon lemon juice
½ tablespoon ground chili

1. Combine the breadcrumbs, salt, pepper, and garlic in a mixing bowl and lay out on a platter. 2. Roll the chicken in the breadcrumb mixture after brushing it with olive oil. 3. Arrange the chicken in the AirFryer Basket. Place the Air Fryer Basket onto the Baking Pan and insert into rack Position 2. Set the Function Dial to Air Fry. Set Temperature Dial to 400 degrees F, and then turn the ON/Oven Timer dial to 12 minutes. Let the Cuisinart Air Fryer Oven work. 4. Flip the food halfway through. To make the aioli, whisk together mayonnaise, lemon juice, and ground chili. 5. Serve the chicken with aioli that is still hot.
Per serving: Calories 311; Fat 11g; Sodium 780mg; Carbs 22g; Fiber 0.1g; Sugar 0.1g; Protein 31g

Rubbed Chicken Thigh

Prep time: 10 minutes | Cook time: 35 minutes | Serves: 6

6 chicken thighs
For Rub:
½ teaspoon basil
½ teaspoon oregano
½ teaspoon pepper

1 tablespoon olive oil

1 teaspoon garlic powder
1 teaspoon onion powder
½ teaspoon salt

1. Brush the chicken thighs with olive oil. Combine the rub ingredients in a small dish and rub all over the chicken. 2. Place the chicken thighs in the Baking Pan. Insert the Baking Pan into rack Position 1. Set the Function Dial to Bake. 3. Set Temperature Dial to 365 degrees F, and then turn the ON/Oven Timer dial to 30 minutes. 4. Let the Cuisinart Air Fryer Oven work. Serve and have fun.
Per serving: Calories 250; Fat 19g; Sodium 680mg; Carbs 0.9g; Fiber 0.1g; Sugar 0.1g; Protein 18g

Classic Chicken Breasts

Prep time: 10 minutes | Cook time: 30 minutes | Serves: 4

1-pound chicken breasts, skinless and boneless
For marinade:

½ teaspoon dill
1 teaspoon onion powder
¼ teaspoon basil
¼ teaspoon oregano
3 garlic cloves, minced

1 tablespoon lemon juice
3 tablespoons olive oil
¼ teaspoon pepper
½ teaspoon salt

1. Combine all of the marinade ingredients in a mixing dish. Coat the chicken with the marinade well. Refrigerate the bowl overnight after covering it. 2. Transfer the food to the Baking Pan. Insert the Baking Pan into rack Position 1. Set the Function Dial to Bake. 3. Set Temperature Dial to 390 degrees F, and then turn the ON/Oven Timer dial to 30 minutes. Let the Cuisinart Air Fryer Oven work. 4. Serve and have fun.
Per serving: Calories 313; Fat 19g; Sodium 770mg; Carbs 20g; Fiber 1g; Sugar 0.1g; Protein 33g

Chicken Breast

Prep time: 10 minutes | Cook time: 15 minutes | Serves: 8

4 chicken breasts, skinless and boneless
For Rub:

1 teaspoon garlic powder
1 teaspoon onion powder
4 teaspoons brown sugar

1 tablespoon olive oil

4 teaspoons paprika
1 teaspoon black pepper
1 teaspoon salt

1. Olive oil should be brushed on the chicken breasts. 2. Combine the rub ingredients in a small dish and massage all over the chicken breasts. Place the chicken in the Baking Pan. 3. Insert the Baking Pan into rack Position 1. Set the Function Dial to Bake. Set Temperature Dial to 365 degrees F, and then turn the ON/Oven Timer dial to 15 minutes. 4. Let the Cuisinart Air Fryer Oven work. The chicken should reach an internal temperature of 165 degrees F. 5. Serve and have fun.
Per serving: Calories 165; Fat 7.3g; Sodium 600mg; Carbs 2.7g; Fiber 0.1g; Sugar 1.8g; Protein 21.4g

Broccoli Bacon Chicken

Prep time: 10 minutes | Cook time: 30 minutes | Serves: 4

4 chicken breasts, skinless and boneless
⅓ cup mozzarella cheese, shredded
1 cup cheddar cheese, shredded

½ cup ranch dressing
5 bacon slices, cooked and chopped
2 cups broccoli florets, blanched and chopped

1. Place the chicken in the Baking Pan. Bacon and broccoli go on top. Top the chicken with ranch dressing and shredded mozzarella and cheddar cheese. 2. Insert the Baking Pan into rack Position 1. Set the Function Dial to Bake. Set Temperature Dial to 365 degrees F, and then turn the ON/Oven Timer dial to 30 minutes. 3. Let the Cuisinart Air Fryer Oven work. Serve and have fun.
Per serving: Calories 551; Fat 30.8g; Sodium 650mg; Carbs 5.4g; Fiber 0.1g; Sugar 1.7g; Protein 60.4g

Savory Chicken Legs

Prep time: 10 minutes | Cook time: 50 minutes | Serves: 10

10 chicken legs
½ teaspoon ground nutmeg
½ teaspoon ground cinnamon
1 teaspoon ground allspice
1 teaspoon black pepper
1 tablespoon fresh thyme
1½ tablespoons brown sugar

¼ cup soy sauce
⅓ cup fresh lime juice
1 tablespoon ginger, sliced
2 habanero peppers, remove the stem
4 garlic cloves, peeled and smashed
6 green onions, chopped

1. Place the chicken in a big zip to lock bag. 2. In a food processor, combine the remaining ingredients and pulse until combined. Pour the sauce over the chicken. 3. Refrigerate the chicken overnight after sealing the bag and shaking it thoroughly to coat it. 4. Then place the marinated chicken in the baking pan. Insert the Baking Pan into rack Position 1. Set the Function Dial to Bake. Set Temperature Dial to 365 degrees F, and then turn the ON/Oven Timer dial to 50 minutes. Let the Cuisinart Air Fryer Oven work. 5. Serve and have fun.

Per serving: Calories 232; Fat 14.2g; Sodium 586mg; Carbs 4.8g; Fiber 1g; Sugar 2.2g; Protein 21.9g

Protein Baked Chicken

Prep time: 10 minutes | Cook time: 25 minutes | Serves: 6

6 chicken breasts, skinless and boneless
¼ teaspoon paprika
½ teaspoon garlic salt

1 teaspoon Italian seasoning
2 tablespoons olive oil
¼ teaspoon pepper

1. Brush the chicken with olive oil. Rub the chicken with a mixture of Italian spice, garlic salt, paprika, and pepper, and then place the food in the Baking Pan. 2. Insert the Baking Pan into rack Position 1. Set the Function Dial to Bake. Set Temperature Dial to 365 degrees F, and then turn the ON/Oven Timer dial to 25 minutes. Let the Cuisinart Air Fryer Oven work. 3. The meat should reach an internal temperature of 165 degrees F. Cut the meat into slices and serve.

Per serving: Calories 321; Fat 15.7g; Sodium 677mg; Carbs 0.4g; Fiber 0.1g; Sugar 0.1g; Protein 42.3g

Balsamic Flavored Chicken Breasts

Prep time: 10 minutes | Cook time: 25 minutes | Serves: 4

4 chicken breasts, skinless and boneless
2 teaspoons dried oregano
2 garlic cloves, minced
½ cup balsamic vinegar

2 tablespoons soy sauce
¼ cup olive oil
Pepper and salt

1. Combine soy sauce, oil, black pepper, oregano, garlic, and vinegar in a mixing bowl. 2. Pour the soy sauce mixture over the chicken in the Baking Pan. Insert the Baking Pan into rack Position 1. Set the Function Dial to Bake. 3. Set Temperature Dial to 390 degrees F, and then turn the ON/Oven Timer dial to 25 minutes. Let the Cuisinart Air Fryer Oven work. 4. Serve and have fun.

Per serving: Calories 401; Fat 23.5g; Sodium 667mg; Carbs 1.9g; Fiber 0.1g; Sugar 0.3g; Protein 42.9g

Easy Chicken Thighs

Prep time: 10 minutes | Cook time: 35 minutes | Serves: 6

6 chicken thighs
2 teaspoons poultry seasoning

2 tablespoons olive oil
Pepper and salt

1. Brush the chicken with oil and season with salt, pepper, and poultry spice. Place the chicken thighs in the Baking Pan. 2. Insert the Baking Pan into rack Position 1. Set the Function Dial to Bake. Set Temperature Dial to 365 degrees F, and then turn the ON/Oven Timer dial to 35 minutes. 3. Let the Cuisinart Air Fryer Oven work. The meat should reach an internal temperature of 165 degrees F. 4. Serve and have fun.
Per serving: Calories 319; Fat 15.5g; Sodium 558mg; Carbs 0.3g; Fiber 0.1g; Sugar 0.1g; Protein 42.3g

Buffalo Chicken Tenders

Prep time: 60 minutes | Cook time: 25 minutes | Serves: 5

Nonstick cooking spray
⅔ cup panko bread crumbs
½ teaspoon cayenne pepper
½ teaspoon paprika
½ teaspoon garlic powder

½ teaspoon salt
3 chicken breasts, boneless, skinless and cut in 10 strips
½ cup butter, melted
½ cup hot sauce

1. Combine bread crumbs and spices in a shallow dish. Coat the chicken in the crumb mixture on all sides. 2. Refrigerate for 1 hour after placing on prepared pan. Whisk together butter and spicy sauce in a small bowl. 3. Select Bake function. Spray the cooking tray lightly with cooking spray and line it with foil. 4. Place each piece of chicken in the Air Fryer Basket after dipping it in the butter mixture. Place the Air Fryer Basket onto the Baking Pan and insert into rack Position 2. Set the Function Dial to Air Fry. 5. Set Temperature Dial to 400 degrees F, and then turn the ON/Oven Timer dial to 25 minutes. Let the Cuisinart Air Fryer Oven work. Turn the food halfway through. 6. Cook until the chicken is no longer pink and the exterior is crispy and golden brown. Serve right away.
Per serving: Calories 371; Fat 23g; Sodium 777mg; Carbs 10g; Fiber 1g; Sugar 1g; Protein 31g

Chicken Breasts

Prep time: 5 minutes | Cook time: 14 minutes | Serves: 4

½ teaspoon garlic powder
1 teaspoon salt
½ teaspoon freshly ground black pepper

1 teaspoon dried parsley
2 tablespoons olive oil, divided
3 boneless, skinless chicken breasts

1. Combine the garlic powder, salt, pepper, and parsley in a small mixing bowl. Rub each chicken breast with 1 tablespoon of olive oil and half of the spice mix. 2. Place the chicken breasts in the Air Fryer Basket. Place the Air Fryer Basket onto the Baking Pan and insert into rack Position 2. Set the Function Dial to Air Fry. 3. Set Temperature Dial to 370 degrees F, and then turn the ON/Oven Timer dial to 14 minutes. Let the Cuisinart Air Fryer Oven work. 4. Flip the meat and brush the meat with the remaining olive oil and seasonings halfway through. Check that the chicken has achieved a temperature of 165 degrees F on the inside. 5. If necessary, increase the cooking time. Transfer the chicken to a dish and serve after it is thoroughly done.
Per serving: Calories 182; Fat 9g; Sodium 657mg; Carbs 3.2g; Fiber 0.1g; Sugar 0.1g; Protein 26g

Lemon Chicken Thighs

Prep time: 5 minutes | Cook time: 10 minutes | Serves: 4

1 teaspoon salt

1 teaspoon freshly ground black pepper

2 tablespoons olive oil

2 tablespoons Italian seasoning

2 tablespoons freshly squeezed lemon juice

1 lemon, sliced

1. Season the chicken thighs with salt and pepper and place them in a medium mixing basin. 2. Toss the chicken thighs with olive oil, Italian seasoning, and lemon juice until they are well coated in oil. 3. Add the lemon slices. Place the chicken thighs in a single layer in the AirFryer Basket. Place the Air Fryer Basket onto the Baking Pan and insert into rack Position 2. Set the Function Dial to Air Fry. Set Temperature Dial to 400 degrees F, and then turn the ON/Oven Timer dial to 10 minutes. Let the Cuisinart Air Fryer Oven work. 4. After 10 minutes, flip the chicken using tongs. 5. Cook for another 10 minutes after resetting the timer. Check that the chicken has achieved a temperature of 165 degrees F on the inside. 6. If necessary, increase the cooking time. Plate, serve, and enjoy the chicken after it's thoroughly cooked.

Per serving: Calories 325; Fat 26g; Sodium 670mg; Carbs 1g; Fiber 0.1g; Sugar 1g; Protein 20g

Hone Chicken in Wine

Prep time: 5 minutes | Cook time: 15 minutes | Serves: 4

2 chicken breasts, rinsed and halved

1 tablespoon melted butter

½ teaspoon freshly ground pepper, or to taste

¾ teaspoon sea salt, or to taste

1 teaspoon paprika

1 teaspoon dried rosemary

2 tablespoons dry white wine

1 tablespoon honey

1. Blot the chicken breasts dry using a paper towel. Using the melted butter, lightly coat them. 2. After that, combine the remaining ingredients. Place them in the Baking Pan. 3. Insert the Baking Pan into rack Position 1. Set the Function Dial to Bake. Set Temperature Dial to 365 degrees F, and then turn the ON/Oven Timer dial to 15 minutes. 4. Let the Cuisinart Air Fryer Oven work. Serve warm.

Per serving: Calories 189; Fat 14g; Sodium 568mg; Carbs 3.2g; Fiber 0.1g; Sugar 1g; Protein 11g

Ham and Chicken Fillet

Prep time: 5 minutes | Cook time: 15 minutes | Serves: 4

2 large chicken fillets

freshly ground black pepper

4 small slices of brie (or your cheese of choice)

1 tablespoon freshly chopped chives

4 slices cured ham

1. Cut the fillets into four pieces and make incisions like a hamburger bun. At the rear, leave a little "hinge" uncut. Season the interior and stuff it with brie and chives. 2. Put a piece of ham around each one. Brush them with oil before placing them in the Air Fryer Basket. 3. Place the Air Fryer Basket onto the Baking Pan and insert into rack Position 2. Set the Function Dial to Air Fry. Set Temperature Dial to 400 degrees F, and then turn the ON/Oven Timer dial to 15 minutes. 4. Let the Cuisinart Air Fryer Oven work. Cook the little packages until they appear to be delicious. 5. Serve hot.

Per serving: Calories 375; Fat 18.3g; Sodium 553mg; Carbs 0.8g; Fiber 0.1g; Sugar 0.1g; Protein 49.2g

Spiced Chicken with Sweet Potato

Prep time: 5 minutes | Cook time: 55 minutes | Serves: 2

½ teaspoon cayenne pepper
200 ml buttermilk
1 teaspoon garlic, minced
2 pieces chicken breast fillet
4 tablespoons flour
Salt and pepper to taste

1 egg, beaten
8 ounces panko breadcrumbs
2 sweet potatoes, sliced into chips
1 tablespoon sweet smoked paprika
1 tablespoon olive oil

1. Combine the cayenne pepper, buttermilk, and garlic in a mixing bowl. Marinate chicken breasts for 2 hours or overnight in this mixture. 2. Combine the flour, salt and pepper. Using seasoned flour, dredge the chicken. Coat them with breadcrumbs after dipping in the beaten egg. 3. Transfer the chicken to the Air Fryer Basket. Place the Air Fryer Basket onto the Baking Pan and insert into rack Position 2. Set the Function Dial to Air Fry. 4. Set Temperature Dial to 400 degrees F, and then turn the ON/Oven Timer dial to 20 minutes. Let the Cuisinart Air Fryer Oven work. 5. Flip the meat once or twice during cooking to ensure uniform cooking. Serve the chicken with sweet potatoes on the side.
Per serving: Calories 934; Fat 16g; Sodium 980mg; Carbs 79.5g; Fiber 6.5g; Sugar 5.4g; Protein 58.4g

Avocado Chicken Mix

Prep time: 5 minutes | Cook time: 20 minutes | Serves: 2

2 cups chicken
½ avocado (sliced)
Salt and pepper to taste

2 radish (sliced)
Parsley (chopped) for dressing

1. Slice the chicken and toss it into the bowl. Place the radish slices and avocado slices on top of the chicken. 2. When it's done, add the parsley and stir it in. Place the food in the Air Fryer Basket. 3. Place the Air Fryer Basket onto the Baking Pan and insert into rack Position 2. Set the Function Dial to Air Fry. 4. Set Temperature Dial to 400 degrees F, and then turn the ON/Oven Timer dial to 14 minutes. Let the Cuisinart Air Fryer Oven work. 5. When the salad is done, season it with salt and pepper before serving.
Per serving: Calories 227; Fat 8g; Sodium 200mg; Carbs 19g; Fiber 7g; Sugar 11g; Protein 20g

Coconut Chicken Legs

Prep time: 5 minutes | Cook time: 27 minutes | Serves: 3

1 ½ ounces coconut milk
3 teaspoons ginger, grated
4 teaspoons ground turmeric

½ teaspoon sea salt
3 chicken legs (skin removed)

1. Combine the coconut milk, ginger, turmeric, and salt in a large mixing bowl. Make a few slits in the flesh of the bird. 2. Marinate the chicken for 4 hours in the mixture. Store the meat in the refrigerator. Transfer the food to the Air Fryer Basket. 3. Place the Air Fryer Basket onto the Baking Pan and insert into rack Position 2. Set the Function Dial to Air Fry. 4. Set Temperature Dial to 400 degrees F, and then turn the ON/Oven Timer dial to 20 minutes. Let the Cuisinart Air Fryer Oven work. 5. Flip the chicken legs halfway through. Serve warm.
Per serving: Calories 112; Fat 6.5g; Sodium 390mg; Carbs 4g; Fiber 0.1g; Sugar 0.1g; Protein 9.6g

Crunchy Chicken Strips

Prep time: 5 minutes | Cook time: 25 minutes | Serves: 4

12 ounces chicken breast, cut into strips
Salt and pepper to taste
1 egg, beaten

¼ cup whole wheat flour
½ cup panko breadcrumbs
¼ cup curry powder

1. Sprinkle the salt and pepper over the chicken pieces. Each chicken strip should be floured first, and then dipped in the egg. 2. Combine the curry powder and breadcrumbs in a mixing dish. Using the curry powder mixture, coat each of the chicken strips. 3. Place the chicken strips in the Air Fryer Basket. Place the Air Fryer Basket onto the Baking Pan and insert into rack Position 2. Set the Function Dial to Air Fry. 4. Set Temperature Dial to 400 degrees F, and then turn the ON/Oven Timer dial to 15 minutes. Let the Cuisinart Air Fryer Oven work. 5. Flip the chicken strips after 10 minutes of cooking time. Serve warm after cooking.
Per serving: Calories 170; Fat 4.1g; Sodium 477mg; Carbs 11.4g; Fiber 1g; Sugar 1.4g; Protein 21.2g

Orange Chicken

Prep time: 5 minutes | Cook time: 30 minutes | Serves: 4

Olive oil to mist
1 sliced red onion
1 bell pepper, yellow
¾ pound chicken thighs
3 teaspoons curry powder

1 tablespoon cornstarch
¼ cup orange juice
2 tablespoons honey
¼ cup chicken stock

1. In the Air Fryer Basket, place the red onion, pepper, and chicken thighs, and drizzle with olive oil. 2. Place the Air Fryer Basket onto the Baking Pan and insert into rack Position 2. Set the Function Dial to Air Fry. 3. Set Temperature Dial to 400 degrees F, and then turn the ON/Oven Timer dial to 12 minutes. Let the Cuisinart Air Fryer Oven work. Flip the food halfway through. 4. Remove the veggies and chicken from the basket and place them on a plate to the side. 5. Combine the curry powder, cornstarch, orange juice, honey, and stock in a metal bowl and stir well. Toss in the veggies and chicken. 6. Air-Fry them at 400 degrees F for 10 minutes until the sauce is thick and bubbling. Serve.
Per serving: Calories 230; Fat 7g; Sodium 478mg; Carbs 16g; Fiber 1g; Sugar 2g; Protein 26g

Spicy Chicken Breast

Prep time: 5 minutes | Cook time: 25 minutes | Serves: 4

1 teaspoon olive oil
1-pound chicken breast; skinless, boneless
½ cup chicken stock
2 tablespoons curry paste
1 onion diced

2 tablespoons minced garlic
1 tablespoon apple cider vinegar
1 tablespoon lemongrass
½ cup coconut milk

1. Chicken breasts should be cut into cubes. Peel and dice the onion. Mix the chicken cubes and chopped onion in the Air Fryer Basket. 2. Place the Air Fryer Basket onto the Baking Pan and insert into rack Position 2. Set the Function Dial to Air Fry. 3. Set Temperature Dial to 400 degrees F, and then turn the ON/Oven Timer dial to 5 minutes. Let the Cuisinart Air Fryer Oven work. 4. In a separate bowl, combine the minced garlic, apple cider vinegar, lemongrass, coconut milk, chicken stock, and curry paste. 5. Using a wooden spatula, combine the ingredients. Continue to cook the chicken curry for another 10 minutes at the same temperature of Air Fry function. 6. Remove the chicken curry from the air fryer when the timer goes off and it is done cooking. 7. Place the dish on the serving plates now.
Per serving: Calories 275; Fat 15g; Sodium 569mg; Carbs 7.2g; Fiber 1g; Sugar 0.1g; Protein 25.6g

Delicious Chicken

Prep time: 5 minutes | Cook time: 30 minutes | Serves: 4

15 ounces chicken
1 Pandan leaf
½ onion diced
1 teaspoon turmeric
1 tablespoon butter
¼ cup coconut milk

1 tablespoon chives
1 teaspoon minced garlic
1 teaspoon chili flakes
1 teaspoon Stevie
1 teaspoon ground black pepper

1. The chicken should be cut into four large pieces. In a large mixing basin, place the chicken chunks. 2. Mix the minced garlic, chopped onion, chili flakes, Stevie, ground black pepper, chives, and turmeric into the chicken. 3. Combine the meat. Chop the Pandan leaf into four pieces. Pandan leaf is used to wrap the chicken cubes. 4. Place the wrapped chicken in a dish with the coconut milk and let aside for 10 minutes. Place the chicken in the AirFryer Basket. 5. Place the AirFryer Basket onto the Baking Pan and insert into rack Position 2. Set the Function Dial to Air Fry. Set Temperature Dial to 400 degrees F, and then turn the ON/Oven Timer dial to 10 minutes. Let the Cuisinart Air Fryer Oven work. 6. When the chicken is done, move it to serving dishes and refrigerate for at least 2 to 3 minutes before serving.
Per serving: Calories 250; Fat 12.6g; Sodium 750mg; Carbs 3.1g; Fiber 0.1g; Sugar 0.1g; Protein 29.9g

Rosemary Chicken Thighs

Prep time: 5 minutes | Cook time: 27 minutes | Serves: 2

2 chicken thighs (skin removed)
Sea salt and pepper to taste
1 tablespoon lemon juice

3 teaspoons dried rosemary
3 cloves garlic, crushed and minced
1 teaspoon olive oil

1. Season the chicken thighs with sea salt, pepper, lemon juice, and dried rosemary. Marinate the meat for 1 hour. Heat the olive oil and sauté the smashed garlic. 2. Cook the chicken thighs in the Cuisinart Air Fryer Oven at 400 degrees F for 12 minutes on Air Fry mode. 3. Flip the chicken halfway through. Drizzle the garlic oil over the chicken before serving.
Per serving: Calories 188; Fat 12.3g; Sodium 450mg; Carbs 3.2g; Fiber 0.1g; Sugar 0.1g; Protein 16g

Chicken Vegetable Pie

Prep time: 5 minutes | Cook time: 31 minutes | Serves: 8 to 10

2 chicken thighs (boneless, sliced into cubes)
1 teaspoon reduced to sodium soy sauce
1 onion, diced
1 carrot, diced
2 potatoes, diced
1 cup mushrooms

1 teaspoon garlic powder
1 teaspoon flour
½ cup milk
2 hard to boiled eggs, sliced in half
2 sheets puff pastry

1. Season the chicken cubes with the low sodium soy sauce. Sauté the onions, carrots, and potatoes in a pan over low heat. 2. Combine the chicken cubes and mushrooms in a large mixing bowl. Add the garlic powder, flour, and milk and season with salt and pepper. Mix them thoroughly. 3. Place the pastry sheet on the cooking tray. Use a fork to poke holes in it. On top of the pastry sheet, arrange the eggs. On top of the eggs, pour the chicken mixture. 4. Place the second pastry layer on top. Press a little harder. Cook the chicken thighs in the Cuisinart Air Fryer Oven at 400 degrees F for 6 minutes on Air Fry mode. 5. Serve by slicing into numerous pieces.
Per serving: Calories 114; Fat 3.4g; Sodium 500mg; Carbs 9.7g; Fiber 2g; Sugar 1.9g; Protein 11.2g

Turkey Breast with Fresh Spices

Prep time: 10 minutes | Cook time: 40 minutes | Serves: 6

2 ¾ pounds turkey breast
2 tablespoons unsalted butter
1 tablespoon chopped fresh rosemary
1 teaspoon chopped fresh chives

1 teaspoon minced fresh garlic
¼ teaspoon black pepper
½ teaspoon salt

1. Combine chives, rosemary, garlic, salt, and pepper in a mixing bowl. Using a pastry cutter to cut in the butter and mash until thoroughly combined. 2. Rub the herbed butter all over the turkey breast and then place in the Air Fryer Basket on the Baking Pan. 3. Cook the chicken thighs in the Cuisinart Air Fryer Oven at 400 degrees F for 40 minutes on Air Fry mode. 4. Flip the meat halfway through. Wrap the cooked turkey in aluminum foil and let it to rest for at least 10 minutes before slicing. 5. Warm the dish before serving.
Per serving: Calories 263; Fat 10.1g; Sodium 290mg; Carbs 0.3g; Fiber 0.1g; Sugar 0.1g; Protein 40.2g

Lemon Chicken Breasts

Prep time: 10 minutes | Cook time: 15 minutes | Serves: 4

4 boneless skinless chicken breasts
½ teaspoon organic cumin
1 teaspoon sea salt (real salt)
¼ teaspoon black pepper
½ cup butter, melted

1 lemon, ½ juiced, ½ thinly sliced
1 cup chicken bone broth
1 can pitted green olives
½ cup red onions, sliced

1. Season the chicken breasts liberally with salt, cumin, and black pepper. Brush the chicken breasts with melted butter and then place in the Air Fryer Basket on the Baking Pan. 2. Cook the chicken thighs in the Cuisinart Air Fryer Oven at 400 degrees F for 15 minutes on Air Fry mode. Add the remaining ingredients after 5 minutes of cooking time. 3. Serve immediately!
Per serving: Calories 310; Fat 9.4g; Sodium 660mg; Carbs 10.2g; Fiber 3g; Sugar 1.5g; Protein 21.8g

Whole Chicken Wings with Lemon Pepper

Prep time: 10 minutes | Cook time: 20 minutes | Serves: 4

8 whole chicken wings
½ Lemon Juice
½ teaspoon garlic powder
1 teaspoon onion powder

Salt and pepper
¼ cup low to fat buttermilk
½ cup all to purpose flour
Cooking oil

1. Place the wings in a plastic bag that can be sealed. Drizzle lemon juice over the wings. Garlic powder, onion powder, and salt and pepper to taste should be used to season the wings. Close the bag. 2. To mix the ingredients and coat the wings, give it a good shake. Fill separate basins with buttermilk and flour large enough to dip the wings in. 3. Cooking oil should be sprayed on the Air Fryer Basket. Dip the wings in buttermilk and then flour one at a time. Place the wings in the Air Fryer Basket. 4. Place the Air Fryer Basket onto the Baking Pan and insert into rack Position 2. Set the Function Dial to Air Fry. Set Temperature Dial to 400 degrees F, and then turn the ON/Oven Timer dial to 20 minutes. 5. Let the Cuisinart Air Fryer Oven work. Flip the chicken wings every 5 minutes. 6. Allow the dish to cool before serving.
Per serving: Calories 347; Fat 12g; Sodium 440mg; Carbs 1g; Fiber 1g; Sugar 0.1g; Protein 46g

Cheese Chicken Breast Halves

Prep time: 10 minutes | Cook time: 35 minutes | Serves: 4

Nonstick cooking spray
½ cup flour
2 eggs
⅔ cup panko bread crumbs
⅔ cup Italian seasoned bread crumbs
⅓ + ¼ cup parmesan cheese, divided

2 tablespoons fresh parsley, chopped
½ teaspoon salt
¼ teaspoon pepper
4 chicken breast halves, skinless and boneless
24 ounces marinara sauce
1 cup mozzarella cheese, grated

1. Spray the Baking Pan lightly with cooking spray. Fill a small dish halfway with flour. 2. Beat the eggs in a separate shallow bowl. Combine both bread crumbs, ⅓ cup parmesan cheese, 2 tablespoons parsley, salt, and pepper in a third shallow dish. 3. Pound the chicken between two pieces of plastic wrap to a thickness of 1 to 2 inches. 4. To coat the chicken, first coat it in flour, then in eggs, and finally in the bread crumb mixture. 5. Place the items in the pan. Insert the Baking Pan into rack Position 1. Set the Function Dial to Bake. Set Temperature Dial to 365 degrees F, and then turn the ON/Oven Timer dial to 10 minutes. 6. Let the Cuisinart Air Fryer Oven work. Flip the food halfway through. Remove the chicken from the air fryer oven. In the bottom of the pan, pour ½ cup marinara. 7. Place the chicken on top of the sauce and top with another 2 tablespoons of marinara. 8. Add mozzarella and parmesan cheese on the top of the chicken. Bake the food at 365 degrees F for 20 to 25 minutes until bubbling and cheese is golden brown. 9. Serve.
Per serving: Calories 529; Fat 13g; Sodium 1437mg; Carbs 52g; Fiber 5g; Sugar 9g; Protein 51g

Fried Chicken Wings

Prep time: 10 minutes | Cook time: 25 minutes | Serves: 3

1 ½ pounds chicken wings
⅓ cup grated Parmesan cheese
⅓ cup breadcrumbs
⅛ teaspoon garlic powder

⅛ teaspoon onion powder
¼ cup melted butter
Salt and black pepper to taste
Cooking spray

1. Spray the Air Fryer Basket with nonstick cooking spray. 2. Combine Parmesan cheese, garlic powder, onion powder, black pepper, breadcrumbs, and salt in a large mixing bowl. Stir everything together thoroughly. 3. One at a time, dip chicken wings into melted butter and then into the bread mixture until completely covered. 4. Arrange the wings on the basket in a single layer. Place the Air Fryer Basket onto the Baking Pan and insert into rack Position 2. Set the Function Dial to Air Fry. 5. Set Temperature Dial to 400 degrees F, and then turn the ON/Oven Timer dial to 20 minutes. Let the Cuisinart Air Fryer Oven work. 6. Flip the chicken wings halfway through. When cooked, the chicken wings should be no longer pink in the middle and the juices should flow clear. 7. Serve warm.
Per serving: Calories 371; Fat 22.6g; Sodium 443mg; Carbs 11.8g; Fiber 1g; Sugar 2g; Protein 27.8g

Leek Tomato Sauce Chicken

Prep time: 10 minutes | Cook time: 20 minutes | Serves: 4

2 large to sized chicken breasts cut in half lengthwise
Salt and ground black pepper, to taste
4 ounces Cheddar cheese, cut into sticks
1 tablespoon sesame oil
1 cup leeks, chopped

2 cloves garlic, minced
⅔ cup roasted vegetable stock
⅔ cup tomato puree
1 teaspoon dried rosemary
1 teaspoon dried thyme

1. Season the chicken breasts with salt & pepper, then lay a slice of Cheddar cheese in the center. 2. Then, with a kitchen string drizzled with sesame oil, knot it and set it aside. 3. In an air fryer to safe bowl, combine the leeks and garlic. Cook the food in the Cuisinart Air Fryer Oven at 400 degrees F for 18 minutes; add the other ingredients after 5 minutes of cooking time. 4. Serve warm after cooking.
Per serving: Calories 257.7; Fat 1.5g; Sodium 90mg; Carbs 40.8g; Fiber 6.2g; Sugar 7.5g; Protein 22.1g

Nutty Chicken Wings

Prep time: 5 minutes | Cook time: 18 minutes | Serves: 4

1 tablespoon fish sauce
1 tablespoon fresh lemon juice
1 teaspoon sugar

12 chicken middle wings cut into half
2 fresh lemongrass stalks, chopped finely
¼ cup unsalted cashews, crushed

1. Combine the fish sauce, lime juice, and sugar in a mixing bowl. Add the wings and thoroughly cover them in the mixture. 2. Refrigerate for 1 to 2 hours to marinate. Place the chicken wings in the AirFryer Basket. 3. Place the AirFryer Basket onto the Baking Pan and insert into rack Position 2. Set the Function Dial to Air Fry. Set Temperature Dial to 400 degrees F, and then turn the ON/Oven Timer dial to 15 minutes. 4. Let the Cuisinart Air Fryer Oven work. Place the wings on plates to serve. 5. Serve with a cashew mixture on top.
Per serving: Calories 233; Fat 20g; Sodium 233mg; Carbs 15g; Fiber 2g; Sugar 11g; Protein 2g

Garlicky Lamb Cutlets

Prep time: 30 minutes | Cook time: 25 minutes | Serves: 2

2 lamb racks (with 3 cutlets per rack)
2 cloves garlic, peeled and thinly sliced
2 long sprigs of fresh rosemary, leaves removed

2 tablespoons wholegrain mustard
1 tablespoon honey
2 tablespoon mint sauce

1. Trim fat and cut slits in the top of the lamb. Insert the garlic and rosemary leaves in the slits and set the lamb aside. 2. Whisk the mustard, honey, and mint sauce together for marinade and brush over the lamb racks. Let the lamb marinade in a fridge for 20 minutes. 3. Spray the Air Fryer Basket with cooking spray and place the marinated lamb rack in it. Place the Air Fryer Basket onto the Baking Pan and insert into rack Position 2. Set the Function Dial to Air Fry. 4. Set Temperature Dial to 360 degrees F, and then turn the ON/Oven Timer dial to 20 minutes. Let the Cuisinart Air Fryer Oven work. 5. Flip the food halfway through. Once done, place the food on a platter and cover with foil to rest for 10 minutes before slicing and serving. 6. Serve warm with your favorite sauce and salad on the side and enjoy.
Per Serving: Calories 248; Fat 10g; Sodium 546mg; Carbs 5g; Fiber 2.1g; Sugar 1g; Protein 45g

Coated Lamb Chops

Prep time: 5 minutes | Cook time: 15 minutes | Serves: 2

1 teaspoon oregano
1 teaspoon coriander
1 teaspoon thyme
1 teaspoon rosemary
½ teaspoon salt

¼ teaspoon pepper
2 tablespoons lemon juice
1 tablespoon olive oil
1-pound lamb chops

1. In a resealable bag, add the oregano, coriander, thyme, rosemary, salt, pepper, lemon juice, and olive oil and shake well to mix. 2. Place the chops in the spiced mix bag and squish to toss the chop with the mixture. Refrigerate 1 hour for well marinated. 3. Place the chops in the Air Fryer Basket that has been sprayed with cooking spray. Place the Air Fryer Basket onto the Baking Pan and insert into rack Position 2. Set the Function Dial to Air Fry. 4. Set Temperature Dial to 390 degrees F, and then turn the ON/Oven Timer dial to 7 minutes. Let the Cuisinart Air Fryer Oven work. 5. Flip the food after 3 minutes of cooking time. Serve hot with ranch sauce.
Per Serving: Calories 624; Fat 25g; Sodium 1070mg; Carbs 7g; Fiber 3g; Sugar 0.3g; Protein 58g

Mustard Lamb Chops

Prep time: 10 minutes | Cook time: 15 minutes | Serves: 2

1 tablespoon Dijon mustard
½ tablespoon fresh lemon juice
½ teaspoon olive oil

½ teaspoon dried tarragon
Salt and ground black pepper, as required
4 (4-oz) lamb loin chops

1. Mix the mustard, lemon juice, oil, tarragon, salt, and black pepper in a small bowl. 2. In a bowl, add the chops with the spice mix and coat with the mixture generously. 3. Arrange the chops onto the greased AirFryer Basket. Place the Air Fryer Basket onto the Baking Pan and insert into rack Position 2. Set the Function Dial to Air Fry. Set Temperature Dial to 390 degrees F, and then turn the ON/Oven Timer dial to 15 minutes. Let the Cuisinart Air Fryer Oven work. Cook the chops until tender. 4. Serve hot with sauce.
Per Serving: Calories 543; Fat 23g; Sodium 804mg; Carbs 14g; Fiber 2g; Sugar 3g; Protein 38g

Moroccan Lamb Burgers

Prep time: 10 minutes | Cook time: 20 minutes | Serves: 4

For the Moroccan spice mix:

1 teaspoon ground ginger
1 teaspoon ground cumin
1 teaspoon sea salt
¾ teaspoon ground black pepper
½ teaspoon ground coriander

½ teaspoon ground allspice
½ teaspoon ground cloves
½ teaspoon ground cinnamon
½ teaspoon cayenne

For burgers and dip:

1 ½ pound ground lamb
1 teaspoon Harissa paste
1 tablespoon Moroccan spice mix, divided
1 teaspoon garlic, peeled and minced

¼ teaspoon fresh chopped oregano
1 tablespoon plain Greek yogurt
1 small lemon, juiced

1. In a large bowl, place the lamb and add the Harissa sauce, 1 tablespoon of the Moroccan spice mix, and the garlic. Mix everything with the hands well until incorporated and form 4 patties. 2. Spray the AirFryer Basket with cooking spray and place the burgers in it. Place the AirFryer Basket onto the Baking Pan and insert into rack Position 2. Set the Function Dial to Air Fry. 3. Set Temperature Dial to 360 degrees F, and then turn the ON/Oven Timer dial to 12 minutes. Let the Cuisinart Air Fryer Oven work. 4. Flip the patties halfway through. In a bowl, add freshly chopped oregano with the yogurt, 1 teaspoon of the Moroccan spice mix, and the juice of the lemon. 5. Whisk the sauce well with a fork and divide it into small containers to serve with the burgers when they are done.

Per Serving: Calories 304; Fat 19g; Sodium 754mg; Carbs 12g; Fiber 4g; Sugar 2g; Protein 38g

Roasted Lamb and Root Vegetables

Prep time: 35 minutes | Cook time: 2 hours 10 minutes | Serves: 6

4 cloves garlic,
2 springs fresh rosemary,
4 pounds leg of lamb
Salt and pepper to taste, divided
Medium to sized sweet potatoes, peeled and cut into

wedges
1tablespoon oil, divided
1 cup baby carrots
1 teaspoon butter
2 large red potatoes, cubed

1. Chop the rosemary and the garlic. 2. Cut slits in the top of the lamb and insert slices of garlic and some rosemary in each. Seasoned with salt and pepper as per your taste and set aside to cook after the vegetables are done. 3. Coat the sweet potatoes in olive oil and season with salt and pepper lightly. Spray the AirFryer Basket with cooking spray and put it in the wedges. Place the Air Fryer Basket onto the Baking Pan and insert into rack Position 2. Set the Function Dial to Air Fry. Set Temperature Dial to 400 degrees F, and then turn the ON/Oven Timer dial to 8 minutes. Let the Cuisinart Air Fryer Oven work. 4. Shake and cook another 8 minutes or so. Dump into a bowl and cover with foil. 5. Place the carrots in foil and put the butter on top of them. Enclose them in the foil and place the packet in the air fryer. Cook at 400 degrees F for 20 minutes. 6. Then remove from the air fryer. Coat the basket again with cooking spray. Mix the red potatoes with the oil and salt and pepper to taste. 7. Place in the basket and cook at 400 degrees F for 20 minutes, shaking after 10 minutes. Coat a baking pan with cooking spray. 8. Place the leftover garlic and rosemary in the bottom of the pan and place the lamb on top. 9. Set the air fryer for 380 degrees F and air fry for 1 hour, checking after 30 minutes and 45 minutes to make sure it isn't getting too dark. 10. Increase the air fryer heat to 400 degrees F and cook for 10 to 15 minutes. Once done, remove the roast from the air fryer and set it on a platter. 11. Foil wrap it and rest 10 minutes while you place all the vegetables back in the cooking tray and air fry at 350 degrees F for 8 to 10 minutes or until heated through. 12. Serve lamb with roasted veggies all together with the sauce and enjoy.

Per Serving: Calories 425; Fat 32g; Sodium 648mg; Carbs 10g; Fiber 4.6g; Sugar 2.3g; Protein 28g

Hot Tandoori Lamb

Prep time: 10 minutes | Cook time: 20 minutes | Serves: 4

½ onion, peeled and quartered
5 cloves garlic, peeled
1 slices fresh ginger, peeled
1 teaspoon ground fennel
1 teaspoon Garam Masala

1 teaspoon ground cinnamon
½ teaspoon ground cardamom
½ teaspoon cayenne
1 teaspoon salt
1-pound boneless lamb sirloin steaks

1. Ground the onion, garlic, ginger, fennel, Garam Masala, cinnamon, cardamom, cayenne, and salt in a blender. 2. In a large bowl, place the lamb steaks and slash the meat so the spices will be absorbed well into it. Pour the spice mix over the top of the lamb in a bowl and rub it on both sides of the lamb. 3. Let the meat sit at room temperature for 30 minutes or cover and refrigerate overnight to marinate. 4. Spray the Air Fryer Basket with cooking spray and place lamb steaks in without letting them overlap. 5. Place the Air Fryer Basket onto the Baking Pan and insert into rack Position 2. Set the Function Dial to Air Fry. 6. Set Temperature Dial to 350 degrees F, and then turn the ON/Oven Timer dial to 15 minutes. 7. Let the Cuisinart Air Fryer Oven work. Turn the food after 7 minutes of cooking time. 8. Test with the meat thermometer to make sure they are done. The medium to well will be 150 degrees F. 9. Serve with sauce and roasted veggies if desired.
Per Serving: Calories 542; Fat 23g; Sodium 1052mg; Carbs 12g; Fiber 2g; Sugar 1g; Protein 30g

Greek Lamb Leg with Herbs

Prep time: 25 minutes | Cook time: 1 hour 30 minutes | Serves: 6

3 pounds leg of lamb, bone to in
For the Marinade:
1 tablespoon lemon zest
3 tablespoons lemon juice
3 cloves garlic, minced
1 teaspoon onion powder
For the Herb Dressing:
1 tablespoon lemon juice
¼ cup chopped fresh oregano
1 teaspoon fresh thyme

1 teaspoon fresh thyme
¼ cup fresh oregano
¼ cup olive oil
1 teaspoon ground black pepper

1 tablespoon olive oil
1 teaspoon sea salt
Ground black pepper, to taste

1. Place lamb leg in a large resealable bag. In a small bowl, combine the ingredients for the marinade. Stir to mix well. 2. Pour the marinade mix over the lamb, making sure the meat is completely coated. Seal the bag and place it in the refrigerator for marinating. 3. Marinate the meat for 4 to 6 hours before roasting. Remove the lamb leg from the marinade. Place the lamb leg in the Baking Pan. 4. Insert the Baking Pan into rack Position 1. Set the Function Dial to Bake. Set Temperature Dial to 350 degrees F, and then turn the ON/ Oven Timer dial to 90 minutes. 5. Let the Cuisinart Air Fryer Oven work. Baste the lamb leg with marinade for every 30 minutes. 6. While the lamb is roasting, combine the ingredients for the herb dressing in a bowl. Stir them to mix well. 7. When cooking is complete, remove the lamb leg carefully from the Air Fryer Basket using hot pads or gloves. Cover the dish lightly with aluminum foil and wait for 8 to 10 minutes. 8. Carve the leg in serving sizes and arrange on a platter. Drizzle with herb dressing. 9. Serve immediately and enjoy.
Per Serving: Calories 324; Fat 19g; Sodium 1704mg; Carbs 16g; Fiber 0.3g; Sugar 0.3g; Protein 58g

Lemon Rack of Lamb

Prep time: 15 minutes | Cook time: 3 hours 20 minutes | Serves: 4

1 ½ to 1 ¾ pound Frenched rack of lamb
Salt and pepper to taste
½ cup breadcrumbs
1 teaspoon cumin seed
1 teaspoon ground cumin

½ teaspoon salt
1 teaspoon garlic, peeled and grated
Lemon zest (¼ of a lemon)
1 teaspoon vegetable or olive oil
1 egg, beaten

1. Season the lamb rack well with pepper and salt to taste and set it aside. 2. Combine the breadcrumbs, cumin seed, ground cumin, salt, garlic, lemon zest, and oil in a bowl and set aside. 3. In another bowl, beat the egg well. Dip the lamb rack in the egg and then into the breadcrumb mixture. Spray the Air Fryer Basket and put the crusted lamb rack in. 4. Place the Air Fryer Basket onto the Baking Pan and insert into rack Position 2. Set the Function Dial to Air Fry. 5. Set Temperature Dial to 250 degrees F, and then turn the ON/Oven Timer dial to 25 minutes. Let the Cuisinart Air Fryer Oven work. 6. When the cooking is up, increase temperature to 400 degrees F and cook for another 5 minutes. Check internal temperature to make sure it is 145 degrees F for medium to rare or more. 7. Remove rack when done and cover with foil for 10 minutes before servings. Serve and enjoy.
Per Serving: Calories 325; Fat 19g; Sodium 874mg; Carbs 6g; Fiber 2.5g; Sugar 3g; Protein 41g

Macadamia Lamb

Prep time: 20 minutes | Cook time: 32 minutes | Serves: 4

1 tablespoon olive oil
1 clove garlic, peeled and minced
1 ½ to 1 ¾ pound rack of lamb
Salt and pepper to taste

¾ cups unsalted macadamia nuts
1 tablespoon fresh rosemary, chopped
1 tablespoon breadcrumbs
1 egg, beaten

1. In a small bowl, mix the olive oil and garlic Brush the garlic oil all over the rack of lamb. 2. Season the lamb with salt and pepper to taste. Chop the macadamia nuts as fine as possible and put them in a bowl. 3. Mix the rosemary and breadcrumbs with finely chopped macadamia nuts and set them aside. 4. In another bowl, beat the egg well. Dredge the lamb rack in the egg mixture and then into a nutty breadcrumb mixture. 5. Coat the rack well with the mixture. Spray the Air Fryer Basket with cooking spray and place the rack inside. 6. Place the Air Fryer Basket onto the Baking Pan and insert into rack Position 2. Set the Function Dial to Air Fry. Set Temperature Dial to 250 degrees F, and then turn the ON/Oven Timer dial to 25 minutes. 7. Let the Cuisinart Air Fryer Oven work. When the cooking time is up, increase to 400 degrees F and cook for another 5 to 10 minutes or until done. 8. Cover the dish with foil paper and wait for 10 minutes, uncover and separate into chops and serve with hot sauce or ranch sauce.
Per Serving: Calories 258; Fat 19g; Sodium 745mg; Carbs 12g; Fiber 3.6g; Sugar 0g; Protein 28g

Fried Lamb Chops

Prep time: 10 minutes | Cook time: 12 minutes | Serves: 4

4 lamb chops
1 tablespoon dried thyme
3 tablespoons olive oil

Pepper
Salt

1. In a small bowl, mix oil, thyme, pepper, and salt. Brush lamb chops with oil mixture and place onto the Air Fryer Basket. 2. Place the Air Fryer Basket onto the Baking Pan and insert into rack Position 2. Set the Function Dial to Air Fry. 3. Set Temperature Dial to 390 degrees F, and then turn the ON/Oven Timer dial to 12 minutes. Let the Cuisinart Air Fryer Oven work. 4. Turn the food halfway through. Serve hot and enjoy.
Per Serving: Calories 435; Fat 9.7g; Sodium 870mg; Carbs 5g; Fiber 2g; Sugar 2g; Protein 35g

Herbed Lamb Chops

Prep time: 5 minutes | Cook time: 15 minutes | Serves: 2

4(4-oz, ½ inch thick) lamb loin chops
2 tablespoons fresh rosemary, minced
4 garlic cloves, crushed

¼ teaspoon red chili powder
Salt and ground black pepper, as required

1. Place all ingredients in a bowl and mix well. Marinade the lamb in the refrigerator overnight. 2. Arrange the marinated chops onto the greased baking pan. Insert the Baking Pan into rack Position 1. Set the Function Dial to Bake. Set Temperature Dial to 400 degrees F, and then turn the ON/Oven Timer dial to 15 minutes. Let the Cuisinart Air Fryer Oven work. Flip halfway through the cooking time. Bake the chops until tender. 3. Serve hot with sauce.
Per Serving: Calories 258; Fat 14g; Sodium 1597mg; Carbs 14g; Fiber 1.2g; Sugar 1.3g; Protein 38g

Mint Lamb Meatballs

Prep time: 5 minutes | Cook time: 15 minutes | Serves: 4

1-pound ground lamb
1 egg white
½ teaspoon sea salt
2 tablespoons parsley, fresh, chopped

1 tablespoon coriander, chopped
2 garlic cloves, minced
1 tablespoon olive oil
1 tablespoon mint, chopped

1. In a bowl, add all the ingredients and combine well. Shape small meatballs from the mixture and place them in the Air Fryer Basket. 2. Place the Air Fryer Basket onto the Baking Pan and insert into rack Position 2. Set the Function Dial to Air Fry. 3. Set Temperature Dial to 320 degrees F, and then turn the ON/Oven Timer dial to 15 minutes. 4. Serve the dish hot with fresh salad and sauce.
Per Serving: Calories 304; Fat 29g; Sodium 904mg; Carbs 14g; Fiber 3.6g; Sugar 0.6g; Protein 27g

Lamb Loin Chops with Rosemary Sauce

Prep time: 10 minutes | Cook time: 52 minutes | Serves: 8

8 lamb loin chops
1 small onion, peeled and chopped
For the sauce:
1 onion, peeled and chopped
1 tablespoon rosemary leaves
1 oz. butter
1 oz. plain flour

Salt and black pepper, to taste

6 fl oz. milk
6 fl oz. vegetable stock
2 tablespoons cream, whipping
Salt and black pepper, to taste

1. Place the lamb loin chops along with onion in a baking tray. Season the lamb with salt and black pepper on top as per taste. 2. Place the lamb in the Baking Pan. Insert the Baking Pan into rack Position 1. Set the Function Dial to Bake. 3. Set Temperature Dial to 350 degrees F, and then turn the ON/Oven Timer dial to 45 minutes. Let the Cuisinart Air Fryer Oven work. 4. While meat is baking, prepare the white sauce by melting butter in a saucepan then stir in onions. 5. Sauté the onions for 5 minutes, then stir in the flour and cook for 2 minutes. 6. Put all ingredients in the onion flour mix and stir well until well incorporated in a silky smooth sauce. Pour the sauce over baked chops and serve. 7. Enjoy yummy chops with white creamy sauce.
Per Serving: Calories 254; Fat 12g; Sodium 638mg; Carbs 16g; Fiber 3.6g; Sugar 5g; Protein 24g

Typical Roast Lamb

Prep time: 5 minutes | Cook time: 15 minutes | Serves: 2

10 ounces lamb leg roast, patted dry
1 tablespoon olive oil
1 teaspoon rosemary, fresh or dried

1 teaspoon thyme, fresh or dried
½ teaspoon black pepper
½ teaspoon salt

1. In a large bowl, mix the olive oil, rosemary, black pepper, salt and thyme. 2. Coat the lamb well into the oil mixture. Put the lamb in the Air Fryer Basket. 3. Place the Air Fryer Basket onto the Baking Pan and insert into rack Position 2. Set the Function Dial to Air Fry. 4. Set Temperature Dial to 360 degrees F, and then turn the ON/Oven Timer dial to 15 minutes. Let the Cuisinart Air Fryer Oven work. 5. Check if the lamb is cooked with a meat thermometer – the temperature in the center should be 145 degrees F (medium). 6. Air-fry the dish for 3 more minutes until desired tenderness. Remove the dish from the air fryer oven, cover the dish with foil and let it rest for 5 minutes before serving. 7. Serve warm with sauce and fresh salad as a side and enjoy.
Per Serving: Calories 521; Fat 15g; Sodium 985mg; Carbs 13g; Fiber 6g; Sugar 2g; Protein 45g

Garlicky Lamb Chops

Prep time: 10 minutes | Cook time: 45 minutes | Serves: 8

8 medium lamb chops
¼ cup olive oil
3 thin lemon slices
2 garlic cloves, crushed

1 teaspoon dried oregano
1 teaspoon salt
½ teaspoon black pepper

1. Rub the chops with olive oil in the Baking Pan. Add lemon slices, garlic, oregano, salt, and black pepper on top of the oiled lamb chops. 2. Insert the Baking Pan into rack Position 1. Set the Function Dial to Bake. 3. Set Temperature Dial to 400 degrees F, and then turn the ON/Oven Timer dial to 45 minutes. Let the Cuisinart Air Fryer Oven work. 4. Slice and serve warm.
Per Serving: Calories 404; Fat 12g; Sodium 1504mg; Carbs 2g; Fiber 0.3g; Sugar 0.6g; Protein 25g

Lamb with Veggies

Prep time: 10 minutes | Cook time: 60 minutes | Serves: 6

2 tablespoons canola oil
2 pounds boneless leg of lamb, diced
1 onion, chopped
2 leeks white portion only, sliced
2 carrots, sliced
2 tablespoons minced fresh parsley, divided

½ teaspoon dried rosemary, crushed
½ teaspoon salt
¼ teaspoon black pepper
¼ teaspoon dried thyme, crushed
3 potatoes, peeled and sliced
3 tablespoons butter, melted

1. In the Baking Pan, toss the lamb cubes with all the veggies, oil, and seasonings. Insert the Baking Pan into rack Position 1. Set the Function Dial to Bake. 2. Set Temperature Dial to 350 degrees F, and then turn the ON/Oven Timer dial to 60 minutes. Let the Cuisinart Air Fryer Oven work. 3. Slice and serve warm with ranch sauce and veggies.
Per Serving: Calories 354; Fat 10g; Sodium 844mg; Carbs 6g; Fiber 3.6g; Sugar 6g; Protein 26g

Onion Lamb Kebabs

Prep time: 10 minutes | Cook time: 20 minutes | Serves: 4

18 ounces lamb kebab
1 teaspoon chili powder
1 teaspoon cumin powder

1 egg
2 ounces onion, bite to sized chunks
2 teaspoons sesame oil

1. Whisk the egg with chili powder, oil, cumin powder, and salt in a bowl. Add lamb kebabs and onion chunks to coat well then thread it on the skewers. 2. Place these lamb skewers in the AirFryer Basket. Place the AirFryer Basket onto the Baking Pan and insert into rack Position 2. Set the Function Dial to Air Fry. 3. Set Temperature Dial to 395 degrees F, and then turn the ON/Oven Timer dial to 20 minutes. Let the Cuisinart Air Fryer Oven work. 4. Serve warm with sauce and enjoy.
Per Serving: Calories 254; Fat 9g; Sodium 502mg; Carbs 3g; Fiber 1g; Sugar 0.2g; Protein 28g

Orange Lamb Riblets with Onion

Prep time: 10 minutes | Cook time: 45 minutes | Serves: 4

1 cup parsley
1 cup mint
1 small yellow onion, roughly chopped
⅓ cup pistachios, chopped.
1 teaspoon lemon zest, grated
5 tablespoons olive oil

2 pounds lamb riblets
½ onions, chopped.
5 garlic cloves, minced
Juice from 1 orange
Salt and black pepper to the taste

1. Mix parsley with mint, onion, pistachios, lemon zest, salt, pepper, and oil and blend very well into mint pesto puree. 2. Rub lamb with this pesto sauce, place in a bowl; cover and leave in the fridge for 1 hour to marinate. Transfer lamb to the Air Fryer Basket and adds garlic, drizzle orange juice. 3. Place the Air Fryer Basket onto the Baking Pan and insert into rack Position 2. Set the Function Dial to Air Fry. 4. Set Temperature Dial to 300 degrees F, and then turn the ON/Oven Timer dial to 45 minutes. Let the Cuisinart Air Fryer Oven work. 5. Turn the food halfway through. Serve the dish on a plate with salad and sauce and enjoy.
Per Serving: Calories 652; Fat 20g; Sodium 1986mg; Carbs 15g; Fiber 6g; Sugar 2g; Protein 50g

Boneless Lamb Shoulder

Prep time: 10 minutes | Cook time: 60 minutes | Serves: 2

1-pound boneless lamb shoulder roast
4 cloves garlic, minced
1 tablespoon rosemary, chopped
2 teaspoons thyme leaves

3 tablespoons olive oil, divided
Salt
Black pepper
2 pounds baby potatoes halved

1. In the Baking Pan, toss potatoes with all the herbs, seasonings, and oil. 2. Insert the Baking Pan into rack Position 1. Set the Function Dial to Bake. 3. Set Temperature Dial to 370 degrees F, and then turn the ON/Oven Timer dial to 60 minutes. 4. Let the Cuisinart Air Fryer Oven work. Slice and serve the meat warm with veggies and sauce.
Per Serving: Calories 454; Fat 19g; Sodium 844mg; Carbs 4g; Fiber 1.2g; Sugar 0.3g; Protein 20g

Spiced Lamb Kebabs

Prep time: 10 minutes | Cook time: 60 minutes | Serves: 3

1½ pounds lamb shoulder, bones removed and cut into pieces
2 tablespoons cumin seeds, toasted
2 teaspoons caraway seeds, toasted

1 tablespoon Sichuan peppercorns
1 teaspoon sugar
2 teaspoons crushed red pepper flakes
Salt and pepper

1. In a large bowl, place all ingredients and allow the meat to marinate in the refrigerator for at least 2 hours. 2. Transfer the food to the Baking Pan. Insert the Baking Pan into rack Position 1. Set the Function Dial to Bake. 3. Set Temperature Dial to 390 degrees F, and then turn the ON/Oven Timer dial to 15 minutes. Let the Cuisinart Air Fryer Oven work. 4. Flip the meat every 8 minutes for even roasting. Serve the meat hot with sauce and enjoy.
Per Serving: Calories 522; Fat 12g; Sodium 1184mg; Carbs 6g; Fiber 2.6g; Sugar 3.2g; Protein 24g

Crispy Taquitos

Prep time: 10 minutes | Cook time: 16 minutes | Serves: 5

1 cup shredded cheese of your choice
½ cup diced onions
2 cups shredded meat

Spray cooking oil
1 package corn tortillas
Sour cream, salsa, cheese, and guacamole for garnish

1. Place tortilla bread on a tray or plate. Place a small amount of onion, meat, and cheese on the tortilla and roll around. Make all the rolls with the same procedure. 2. Place the rolled tortillas on the Air Fryer Basket. Place the Air Fryer Basket onto the Baking Pan and insert into rack Position 2. Set the Function Dial to Air Fry. 3. Set Temperature Dial to 350 degrees F, and then turn the ON/Oven Timer dial to 16 minutes. Let the Cuisinart Air Fryer Oven work. 4. Turn the food halfway through. Garnish the dish with guacamole, sour cream, cheese, and onion. 5. Serve warm and enjoy.
Per Serving: Calories 444; Fat 20g; Sodium 1784mg; Carbs 9g; Fiber 2.6g; Sugar 2.3g; Protein 28g

Savory Lamb Chops

Prep time: 10 minutes | Cook time: 10 minutes | Serves: 1

⅓ lb. lamb chop
1 tablespoon fresh thyme, chopped
1 tablespoon fresh rosemary, chopped
½ tablespoon Dijon mustard

½ tablespoon olive oil
Pepper
Salt

1. Mix oil, Dijon mustard, rosemary, thyme, pepper, and salt well in a small bowl. Brush lamb chop with oil mixture and place in the Air Fryer Basket. 2. Place the Air Fryer Basket onto the Baking Pan and insert into rack Position 2. Set the Function Dial to Air Fry. Set Temperature Dial to 375 degrees F, and then turn the ON/Oven Timer dial to 10 minutes. 3. Let the Cuisinart Air Fryer Oven work. Turn the food halfway through. Serve hot with sauce and enjoy.
Per Serving: Calories 252; Fat 9g; Sodium 524mg; Carbs 3g; Fiber 0.23g; Sugar 0.1g; Protein 21g

Mint Lamb Patties

Prep time: 10 minutes | Cook time: 8 minutes | Serves: 4

1-pound ground lamb
6 basil leaves, minced
8 mint leaves, minced
¼ cup fresh parsley, chopped
1 teaspoon dried oregano

1 cup feta cheese, crumbled
1 tablespoon garlic, minced
1 jalapeno pepper, minced
¼ teaspoon pepper
½ teaspoon kosher salt

1. In a large bowl, add all ingredients and mix until well combined. Make the equal shape of patties from seasoned meat mixture and place them onto the parchment to lined Baking Pan. 2. Insert the Baking Pan into rack Position 1. Set the Function Dial to Bake. Set Temperature Dial to 400 degrees F, and then turn the ON/ Oven Timer dial to 16 minutes. 3. Let the Cuisinart Air Fryer Oven work. Flip the food halfway through. 4. Serve the dish with salad and sauce and enjoy.
Per Serving: Calories 374; Fat 11g; Sodium 325mg; Carbs 15g; Fiber 3.6g; Sugar 0.6g; Protein 38g

Fresh Lamb Loin Chops

Prep time: 10 minutes | Cook time: 12 minutes | Serves: 4

4 lamb loin chops
1 tablespoon garlic, chopped
2 tablespoons olive oil
¼ cup lemon juice

¼ teaspoon cayenne pepper
½ teaspoon thyme
1 teaspoon rosemary
1 teaspoon sea salt

1. In a zip lock bag, add lamb chops and remaining ingredients, seal bag, and place in the refrigerator for 1 hour for marinating. 2. Place marinated lamb chops onto the Air Fryer Basket. Place the Air Fryer Basket onto the Baking Pan and insert into rack Position 2. Set the Function Dial to Air Fry. 3. Set Temperature Dial to 390 degrees F, and then turn the ON/Oven Timer dial to 120 minutes. Let the Cuisinart Air Fryer Oven work. 4. Turn the food halfway through. Serve the dish hot with sauce and enjoy.
Per Serving: Calories 351; Fat 9g; Sodium 904mg; Carbs 12g; Fiber 3.6g; Sugar 0g; Protein 32g

Cardamom Lamb Steaks

Prep time: 10 minutes | Cook time: 15 minutes | Serves: 4

1-pound lamb sirloin steaks, bless
1 teaspoon ground fennel
1 teaspoon garam masala
5 garlic cloves
1 tablespoon ginger

1 teaspoon cayenne
½ teaspoon ground cardamom
1 teaspoon ground cinnamon
½ onion
1 teaspoon salt

1. In a blender, add all ingredients except steak and blend until smooth. Add puree mixture and steak into the bowl and coat well. 2. Cover and place the seasoned meat in the refrigerator for 1 hour to marinate. 3. Place marinated meat onto the Air Fryer Basket. Place the Air Fryer Basket onto the Baking Pan and insert into rack Position 2. Set the Function Dial to Air Fry. 4. Set Temperature Dial to 330 degrees F, and then turn the ON/Oven Timer dial to 30 minutes. 5. Let the Cuisinart Air Fryer Oven work. Turn the food halfway through. 6. Serve hot with sauce and enjoy.
Per Serving: Calories 642; Fat 24g; Sodium 1855mg; Carbs 14g; Fiber 1.6g; Sugar 2.3g; Protein 24g

Seasoned Lamb Pieces

Prep time: 10 minutes | Cook time: 10 minutes | Serves: 4

1-pound lamb, cut into 1-inch pieces
2 tablespoons olive oil
½ teaspoon cayenne
2 tablespoons ground cumin

2 chili peppers, chopped
1 tablespoon garlic, minced
1 teaspoon salt

1. In a zip lock bag, add lamb chops and remaining ingredients, seal bag, and place in the refrigerator for 1 hour for marinating. 2. Place marinated meat onto the Air Fryer Basket. Place the Air Fryer Basket onto the Baking Pan and insert into rack Position 2. Set the Function Dial to Air Fry. 3. Set Temperature Dial to 360 degrees F, and then turn the ON/Oven Timer dial to 10 minutes. Let the Cuisinart Air Fryer Oven work. 4. Serve hot and enjoy.

Per Serving: Calories 554; Fat 17g; Sodium 1325mg; Carbs 12g; Fiber 6g; Sugar 0g; Protein 24g

Mutton Galette

Prep time: 10 minutes | Cook time: 25 minutes | Serves: 2

2 tablespoons garam masala
1 pound minced mutton
3 teaspoons ginger finely chopped
1 to 2 tablespoon fresh coriander leaves

2 or 3 green chilies finely chopped
1 ½ tablespoon lemon juice
Salt and pepper to taste

1. In a bowl, mix the ingredients until well incorporated. Mold this mixture into a round and flat French Cuisine Galettes. 2. Wet the French Cuisine Galettes slightly with water to prevent from sticking. Place the French Cuisine Galettes in the Air Fryer Basket. 3. Place the Air Fryer Basket onto the Baking Pan and insert into rack Position 2. Set the Function Dial to Air Fry. Set Temperature Dial to 160 degrees F, and then turn the ON/Oven Timer dial to 25 minutes. 4. Let the Cuisinart Air Fryer Oven work. Keep rolling them over to get a uniform cook. 5. 1Serve either with mint sauce or ketchup and enjoy.

Per Serving: Calories 421; Fat 7.9g; Sodium 604mg; Carbs 7g; Fiber 2g; Sugar 0.3g; Protein 25g

Marinated Lamb Chops

Prep time: 10 minutes | Cook time: 8 minutes | Serves: 4

1-pound lamb chops
1 teaspoon oregano
1 teaspoon thyme
1 teaspoon rosemary

2 tablespoons lemon juice
2 tablespoons olive oil
1 teaspoon coriander
1 teaspoon salt

1. In a zip lock bag, add lamb chops and remaining ingredients, seal bag, and place in the refrigerator for 1 hour for marinating. 2. Place marinated lamb chops onto the Air Fryer Basket. Place the Air Fryer Basket onto the Baking Pan and insert into rack Position 2. Set the Function Dial to Air Fry. 3. Set Temperature Dial to 390 degrees F, and then turn the ON/Oven Timer dial to 8 minutes. Let the Cuisinart Air Fryer Oven work. 4. Turn the food halfway through. Serve the dish with sauce and fresh salad and enjoy.

Per Serving: Calories 534; Fat 19g; Sodium 1704mg; Carbs 13g; Fiber 5g; Sugar 0.13g; Protein 21g

Delicious Lamb Kebab

Prep time: 10 minutes | Cook time: 25 minutes | Serves: 2

3 teaspoons lemon juice
2 teaspoons garam masala
4 tablespoons chopped coriander
3 tablespoons cream
1 pound of lamb
3 onions chopped
5 green chilies to roughly chopped

1½ tablespoons ginger paste
1½ teaspoons garlic paste
1½ teaspoons salt
4 tablespoons fresh mint chopped
3 tablespoons chopped capsicum
3 eggs
2½ tablespoons white sesame seeds

1. Cube the lamb into medium to sized chunks. Marinate lamb chunks overnight in any marinade of your choice. 2. Take the lemon juice, garam masala, coriander, and cream in a bowl and mix them well. Grind them thoroughly to make a smooth paste. 3. In another bowl, crack the eggs and beat them. Add a pinch of salt and leave them aside. Take a flat plate and in it mix the sesame seeds and breadcrumbs. 4. Mold the lamb mixture into small balls and flatten them into a round and flat patties like kebabs. 5. Dip these kebabs in the egg and salt mixture and then in the mixture of breadcrumbs and sesame seeds. 6. Leave these kebabs in the fridge for an hour or so to set. Place the kebabs in the Air Fryer Basket. 7. Place the Air Fryer Basket onto the Baking Pan and insert into rack Position 2. Set the Function Dial to Air Fry. Set Temperature Dial to 160 degrees F, and then turn the ON/Oven Timer dial to 25 minutes. Let the Cuisinart Air Fryer Oven work. 8. Turn the kebabs halfway through. Serve the kebabs with mint sauce and salad.
Per Serving: Calories 321; Fat 7g; Sodium 670mg; Carbs 5g; Fiber 1.6g; Sugar 1g; Protein 21g

Corn Flour Lamb Fries

Prep time: 10 minutes | Cook time: 15 minutes | Serves: 2

2 teaspoons salt
1 teaspoon pepper powder
1 pound b1less lamb cut into Oregano Fingers
2 cups dry breadcrumbs
2 teaspoons oregano
2 teaspoons red chili flakes

1 ½ tablespoon ginger-garlic paste
4 tablespoons lemon juice
1 teaspoon red chili powder
6 tablespoons corn flour
4 eggs

1. In a bowl, mix all the ingredients for the marinade. Put the lamb Oregano Fingers inside marinate and let it rest overnight. 2. Mix the breadcrumbs, oregano, and red chili flakes well. Place the marinated Oregano Fingers on this mixture. 3. Cover it with plastic wrap and leave it till right before you serve to cook. Place the Oregano Fingers in the Air Fryer Basket. 4. Place the Air Fryer Basket onto the Baking Pan and insert into rack Position 2. Set the Function Dial to Air Fry. Set Temperature Dial to 160 degrees F, and then turn the ON/Oven Timer dial to 15 minutes. 5. Let the Cuisinart Air Fryer Oven work. Toss the Oregano Fingers well so that they are cooked uniformly. 6. Serve hot with sauce and enjoy.
Per Serving: Calories 554; Fat 10g; Sodium 1706mg; Carbs 14g; Fiber 3.6g; Sugar 0.6g; Protein 32g

Veggies and Pork Patties

Prep time: 10 minutes | Cook time: 20 minutes | Serves: 5

1-pound ground pork
2 teaspoons butter, melted
1 medium carrot, grated
1 small zucchini, grated

1 bell pepper, chopped
1 small leek, finely chopped
1 teaspoon garlic, minced
1 teaspoon Italian seasoning mix

1. Combine all the ingredients in a large mixing bowl. Shape the meat and veggies mixture into equal patties. 2. Place the patties into the Air Fryer Basket. Place the Air Fryer Basket onto the Baking Pan and insert into rack Position 2. Set the Function Dial to Air Fry. 3. Set Temperature Dial to 370 degrees F, and then turn the ON/Oven Timer dial to 16 minutes. Let the Cuisinart Air Fryer Oven work. 4. Turn the food halfway through. Once done, remove from the air fryer and serve hot with toasted buns and salad. 5. Bon appétit!
Per Serving: Calories 288; Fat 20.2g; Sodium 478mg; Carbs 5.7g; Fiber 1.3g; Sugar 2.3g; Protein 16g

Blade Pork Steaks

Prep time: 10 minutes | Cook time: 32 minutes | Serves: 4

1 ½ pound blade pork steaks
2 tablespoons olive oil
1 teaspoon cayenne pepper
1 teaspoon dried oregano

1 teaspoon dried basil
1 teaspoon dried rosemary
Sea salt and ground black pepper, to taste

1. In a mixing bowl, add all ingredients along with steak and mix well. Marinate the steak for 30 minutes in refrigerator. 2. Place the steak in the AirFryer Basket. Place the AirFryer Basket onto the Baking Pan and insert into rack Position 2. Set the Function Dial to Air Fry. 3. Set Temperature Dial to 360 degrees F, and then turn the ON/Oven Timer dial to 30 minutes. Let the Cuisinart Air Fryer Oven work. 4. Turn the food halfway through. Serve hot with roasted veggies as the side. 5. Bon appétit!
Per Serving: Calories 379; Fat 27.8g; Sodium 623mg; Carbs 0.5g; Fiber 0.3g; Sugar 0g; Protein 29.6g

Chapter 7 Dessert Recipes

Syrup Banana Pieces

Prep time: 10 minutes | Cook time: 10 minutes | Serves: 4

2 ripe bananas, peeled and sliced lengthwise
1 teaspoon fresh lime juice

4 teaspoons maple syrup
⅛ teaspoon ground cinnamon

1. Coat each banana half with lime juice. Arrange the banana pieces in the Air Fryer Basket with cut to side up. 2. Drizzle the banana pieces with maple syrup and sprinkle with cinnamon. Place the Air Fryer Basket onto the Baking Pan and insert into rack Position 2. Set the Function Dial to Air Fry. 3. Set Temperature Dial to 350 degrees F, and then turn the ON/Oven Timer dial to 10 minutes. 4. Let the Cuisinart Air Fryer Oven work. Serve immediately.
Per Serving: Calories 70; Fat 0.2g; Sodium 1mg; Carbs 18g; Fiber 1.6g; Sugar 11.2g; Protein 0.6 g

Sweet Raspberry Roll

Prep time: 20 minutes | Cook time: 25 minutes | Serves: 6

1 tube full to sheet crescent roll dough
4 ounces cream cheese, softened
¼ cup raspberry jam

½ cup fresh raspberries, chopped
1 cup powdered sugar
2 to 3 tablespoons heavy whipping cream

1. Place the sheet of crescent roll dough onto a flat surface and unroll it. In a microwave to safe bowl, add the cream cheese and microwave for about 20 to 30 seconds. 2. Remove from microwave and stir until creamy and smooth. Spread the cream cheese over the dough sheet, followed by the raspberry jam. 3. Place the raspberry pieces evenly across the top. From the short side, roll the dough and pinch the seam to seal. 4. Arrange a greased parchment paper onto the Baking Pan. Carefully curve the rolled pastry into a horseshoe shape and arrange it onto the pan. 5. Insert the Baking Pan into rack Position 1. Set the Function Dial to Bake. Set Temperature Dial to 350 degrees F, and then turn the ON/Oven Timer dial to 25 minutes. 6. Let the Cuisinart Air Fryer Oven work. When cooking time is complete, remove the pan from the Cuisinart Air Fryer Oven and place it onto a rack for cooling. 7. Meanwhile, in a bowl, mix together the powdered sugar and cream. Drizzle the cream mixture over cooled Danish and serve.
Per Serving: Calories 335; Fat 15.3g; Sodium 342mg; Carbs 45.3g; Fiber 0.7g; Sugar 30.1g; Protein 4.4 g

Pecan Blueberry Cupcakes

Prep time: 15 minutes | Cook time: 15 minutes | Serves: 8

¼ cup unsweetened coconut milk
2 large eggs
½ teaspoon vanilla extract
1½ cups almond flour
¼ cup Swerve
1 teaspoon baking powder

¼ teaspoon ground cinnamon
Pinch of ground cloves
Pinch of ground nutmeg
⅛ teaspoon salt
½ cup fresh blueberries
¼ cup pecans, chopped

1. Add the coconut milk, eggs, and vanilla extract in a blender and pulse for about 20 to 30 seconds. Add the almond flour, Swerve, baking powder, spices, and salt, and pulse for about 30 to 45 seconds until well blended. 2. Transfer the mixture to a bowl. Gently fold in half of the blueberries and pecans. Place the mixture into 8 silicone muffin cups and top each with the remaining blueberries. 3. Arrange the muffin cups in the Baking Pan. Insert the Baking Pan into rack Position 1. Set the Function Dial to Bake. 4. Set Temperature Dial to 325 degrees F, and then turn the ON/Oven Timer dial to 15 minutes. Let the Cuisinart Air Fryer Oven work. 5. When cooked, cool the dish for 10 minutes. Carefully invert the muffins onto the wire rack to cool completely before serving.
Per Serving: Calories 191; Fat 16.5g; Sodium 54mg; Carbs 14.8g; Fiber 3.2g; Sugar 9.7g; Protein 6.8 g

Fresh Cranberry Muffins

Prep time: 15 minutes | Cook time: 15 minutes | Serves: 10

4½ ounces self to rising flour
½ teaspoon baking powder
Pinch of salt
½ ounce cream cheese softened
4¾ ounces butter softened

4¼ ounces caster sugar
2 eggs
2 teaspoons fresh lemon juice
½ cup fresh cranberries

1. In a bowl, mix together the flour, baking powder, and salt. In another bowl, mix together the cream cheese and butter. 2. Add the sugar and beat until fluffy and light. Add the eggs, one at a time, and whisk until just combined. Add the flour mixture and stir until well combined. Stir in the lemon juice. 3. Place the mixture into silicone cups and top each with cranberries evenly, pressing slightly. Arrange the cups in the Baking Pan. 4. Insert the Baking Pan into rack Position 1. Set the Function Dial to Bake. Set Temperature Dial to 365 degrees F, and then turn the ON/Oven Timer dial to 15 minutes. 5. Let the Cuisinart Air Fryer Oven work. Carefully invert the cupcakes onto the wire rack to cool completely before serving.
Per Serving: Calories 209; Fat 12.4g; Sodium 110mg; Carbs 22.6g; Fiber 0.6g; Sugar 12.4g; Protein 2.7 g

Almond Zucchini Cake

Prep time: 15 minutes | Cook time: 20 minutes | Serves: 1

¼ cup whole to wheat pastry flour
1 tablespoon sugar
¼ teaspoon baking powder
¼ teaspoon ground cinnamon
Pinch of salt

2 tablespoons plus 2 teaspoons milk
2 tablespoons zucchini, grated and squeezed
2 tablespoons almonds, chopped
1 tablespoon raisins
2 teaspoons maple syrup

1. In a bowl, mix together the flour, sugar, baking powder, cinnamon, and salt. 2. Add the remaining ingredients and mix until well combined. Place the mixture into a lightly greased ramekin. 3. Arrange the ramekin in the Baking Pan. Insert the Baking Pan into rack Position 1. Set the Function Dial to Bake. 4. Set Temperature Dial to 350 degrees F, and then turn the ON/Oven Timer dial to 15 minutes. Let the Cuisinart Air Fryer Oven work. 5. When cooked, cool the dish for a while before serving.
Per Serving: Calories 310; Fat 7g; Sodium 175mg; Carbs 57.5g; Fiber 3.2g; Sugar 27.5g; Protein 7.2 g

Apple Oats

Prep time: 15 minutes | Cook time: 40 minutes | Serves: 2

1½ cups apple, peeled, cored, and sliced
¼ cup sugar, divided
1½ teaspoons cornstarch
3 tablespoons all to purpose flour

¼ teaspoon ground cinnamon
Pinch of salt
1½ tablespoons cold butter, chopped
3 tablespoons rolled oats

1. In a bowl, place apple slices, 1 teaspoon of sugar, and cornstarch and toss to coat well. Divide the plum mixture into lightly greased 2 (8-ounce) ramekins. 2. In a bowl, mix together the flour, remaining sugar, cinnamon, and salt. With 2 forks, blend in the butter until a crumbly mixture forms. 3. Add the oats and gently stir to combine. Place the oat mixture over apple slices into each ramekin. 4. Arrange the ramekins in the Baking Pan. Insert the Baking Pan into rack Position 1. Set the Function Dial to Bake. Set Temperature Dial to 350 degrees F, and then turn the ON/Oven Timer dial to 40 minutes. 5. Let the Cuisinart Air Fryer Oven work. When cooked, cool the dish for 10 minutes before serving.
Per Serving: Calories 337; Fat 9.6g; Sodium 141mg; Carbs 64.3g; Fiber 5.3g; Sugar 42.5g; Protein 2.8 g

Banana Walnut Cake

Prep time: 10 minutes | Cook time: 25 minutes | Serves: 6

1 pound of bananas, mashed
8 ounces flour
6 ounces sugar
3.5 ounces walnuts, chopped

3.5 ounces butter, melted
2 eggs, lightly beaten
¼ teaspoon baking soda

1. Select the Bake function and preheat to 355 degrees F. 2. In a bowl, combine the sugar, butter, egg, flour, and baking soda with a whisk. Stir in the bananas and walnuts. 3. Transfer the mixture to the greased Baking Pan. Insert the Baking Pan into rack Position 1. Set the Function Dial to Bake. 4. Set Temperature Dial to 350 degrees F, and then turn the ON/Oven Timer dial to 25 minutes. 5. Let the Cuisinart Air Fryer Oven work. After 10 minutes, reduce the temperature to 330 degrees F and bake for another 15 minutes. 6. Serve hot.
Per Serving: Calories 70; Fat 0.2g; Sodium 1mg; Carbs 18g; Fiber 1.6g; Sugar 11.2g; Protein 0.6 g

Lemon Apple Pasty

Prep time: 05 minutes | Cook time: 35 minutes | Serves: 4

½ teaspoon vanilla extract
1 beaten egg
1 large apple, chopped
1 Pillsbury Refrigerator pie crust
1 tablespoon butter

1 tablespoon ground cinnamon
1 tablespoon raw sugar
2 tablespoons sugar
2 teaspoons lemon juice
Cooking spray

1. Lightly grease the Baking Pan with cooking spray. Spread the pie crust on the bottom of the pan up to the sides. 2. Mix vanilla, sugar, cinnamon, lemon juice, and apple in a bowl. Pour on top of the pie crust. Top apples with butter slices. 3. Cover apples with the other pie crust. Pierce with a knife the tops of the pie. Spread beaten egg on top of the crust and sprinkle sugar. 4. Insert the Baking Pan into rack Position 1. Set the Function Dial to Bake. Set Temperature Dial to 390 degrees F, and then turn the ON/Oven Timer dial to 35 minutes. 5. Let the Cuisinart Air Fryer Oven work. Decrease the temperature to the 330 degrees F after 25 minutes of cooking time. 6. When cooked, the top should be browned. Serve and enjoy.
Per Serving: Calories 372; Fat 19g; Sodium 190mg; Carbs 5.8g; Fiber 3.6g; Sugar 5g; Protein 4.2 g

Lemon Blueberry Muffins

Prep time: 05 minutes | Cook time: 10 minutes | Serves: 12

1 teaspoon vanilla
Juice and zest of 1 lemon
2 eggs
1 cup blueberries

½ cup cream
¼ cup avocado oil
½ cup monk fruit
2½ cups almond flour

1. Mix monk fruit and flour together. In another bowl, mix vanilla, egg, lemon juice, and cream together. Add mixtures together and blend well. 2. Spoon batter into cupcake holders. Place the mixture into 12 silicone muffin cups. Arrange the muffin cups in the Baking Pan. 3. Insert the Baking Pan into rack Position 1. Set the Function Dial to Bake. Set Temperature Dial to 320 degrees F, and then turn the ON/Oven Timer dial to 10 minutes. 4. Let the Cuisinart Air Fryer Oven work. Carefully, invert the muffins onto the wire rack to completely cool before serving.
Per Serving: Calories 317; Fat 11g; Sodium 190mg; Carbs 5.8g; Fiber 3.6g; Sugar 5g; Protein 3 g

Yummy Banana Muffins

Prep time: 05 minutes | Cook time: 25 minutes | Serves: 12

¾ cup whole wheat flour
¾ cup plain flour
¼ cup cocoa powder
¼ teaspoon baking powder
1 teaspoon baking soda
¼ teaspoon salt

2 large bananas, peeled and mashed
1 cup sugar
⅓ cup canola oil
1 egg
½ teaspoon vanilla essence
1 cup mini chocolate chips

1. In a large bowl, mix together flour, cocoa powder, baking powder, baking soda, and salt. 2. In another bowl, add bananas, sugar, oil, egg and vanilla extract and beat till well combined. Slowly, add flour mixture in egg mixture and mix till just combined. Fold in chocolate chips. Grease 12 muffin tins. 3. Arrange the muffin tins in the Baking Pan. Insert the Baking Pan into rack Position 1. Set the Function Dial to Bake. 4. Set Temperature Dial to 320 degrees F, and then turn the ON/Oven Timer dial to 25 minutes. 5. Let the Cuisinart Air Fryer Oven work. Place the food onto a wire rack to cool for about 10 minutes.
Per Serving: Calories 75; Fat 6.5g; Sodium 342mg; Carbs 45.3g; Fiber 1.7g; Sugar 2g; Protein 1.7 g

Jelly Raspberry Rolls

Prep time: 10 minutes | Cook time: 25 minutes | Serves: 4

1 cup of fresh raspberries, rinsed and patted dry
½ cup of cream cheese softened to room temperature
¼ cup of brown sugar
¼ cup of sweetened condensed milk
1 egg

1 teaspoon of corn starch
6 spring roll wrappers (any brand will do, we like Blue Dragon or Tasty Joy, both available through Target or Walmart, or any large grocery chain)
¼ cup of water

1. Cover the Air Fryer Basket with parchment paper, leaving the edges uncovered to allow air to circulate through the basket. 2. In a mixing bowl, combine the cream cheese, brown sugar, condensed milk, cornstarch, and egg. Beat or whip thoroughly, until all ingredients are completely mixed and fluffy, thick and stiff. Spoon even amounts of the creamy filling into each spring roll wrapper, then top each dollop of filling with several raspberries. 3. Roll up the wraps around the creamy raspberry filling, and seal the seams with a few dabs of water. Place each roll in the basket, seams facing down. 4. Place the Air Fryer Basket onto the Baking Pan and insert into rack Position 2. Set the Function Dial to Air Fry. Set Temperature Dial to 330 degrees F, and then turn the ON/Oven Timer dial to 10 minutes. 5. Let the Cuisinart Air Fryer Oven work. When the cooking time is up, the spring rolls should be golden brown and perfect on the outside, while the raspberries and cream filling will have cooked together in a glorious fusion. 6. Repeat the cooking steps for the rest rolls. Remove with tongs and serve hot or cold.
Per Serving: Calories 335; Fat 15.3g; Sodium 342mg; Carbs 45.3g; Fiber 0.7g; Sugar 30.1g; Protein 4.4 g

Crispy Panko Bananas

Prep time: 05 minutes | Cook time: 10 minutes | Serves: 2

1 cup panko breadcrumbs
3 tablespoons cinnamon
½ cup almond flour

3 egg whites
8 ripe bananas
3 tablespoons vegan coconut oil

1. Heat coconut oil and add breadcrumbs in a saucepan for 2 to 3 minutes until golden. Pour them into bowl. 2. Peel and cut bananas in half. Roll each bananas half into flour, eggs, and crumb mixture. Arrange them in the Air Fryer Basket. 3. Place the Air Fryer Basket onto the Baking Pan and insert into rack Position 2. Set the Function Dial to Air Fry. Set Temperature Dial to 280 degrees F, and then turn the ON/Oven Timer dial to 10 minutes. 4. Let the Cuisinart Air Fryer Oven work. Serve and enjoy.
Per Serving: Calories 219; Fat 10g; Sodium 56mg; Carbs 45.3g; Fiber 1.7g; Sugar 5g; Protein 3 g

Chinese Beignet

Prep time: 10 minutes | Cook time: 8 minutes | Serves: 8

1 tablespoon baking powder
1 tablespoon coconut oil
¾ cup of coconut milk

6teaspoons sugar
2 cups all to purpose flour
½ teaspoon sea salt

1. Mix baking powder, flour, sugar, and salt in a bowl. Add coconut oil and mix well. Add coconut milk and mix until well combined. Knead dough for 3 to 4 minutes. 2. Roll dough half an inch thick and using cookie cutter cut doughnuts. Arrange the doughnuts in the Air Fryer Basket. 3. Place the Air Fryer Basket onto the Baking Pan and insert into rack Position 2. Set the Function Dial to Air Fry. Set Temperature Dial to 375 degrees F, and then turn the ON/Oven Timer dial to 8 minutes. 4. Let the Cuisinart Air Fryer Oven work. Let the dish cool 5 minutes, then transfer to a wire rack and cool completely. 5. Repeat with the rest. Serve and enjoy.
Per Serving: Calories 259; Fat 15.9g; Sodium 56mg; Carbs 27g; Fiber 1.7g; Sugar 5g; Protein 3.8 g

Crusty Bananas with Almond Meal

Prep time: 10 minutes | Cook time: 10 minutes | Serves: 4

4 sliced ripe bananas
1 egg
½ cup breadcrumbs
1½ tablespoons cinnamon sugar

1 tablespoon almond meal
1½ tablespoons coconut oil
1 tablespoon crushed cashew
¼ cup corn flour

1. Add coconut oil over medium heat and add breadcrumbs in the pan and stir for 3 to 4 minutes. 2. Remove pan from heat and transfer breadcrumbs in a bowl. Add almond meal and crush cashew in breadcrumbs and mix well. 3. Dip banana half in corn flour then in egg and finally coat with breadcrumbs. Place coated banana in Air Fryer Basket. 4. Sprinkle them with cinnamon sugar. Place the Air Fryer Basket onto the Baking Pan and insert into rack Position 2. Set the Function Dial to Air Fry. 5. Set Temperature Dial to 350 degrees F, and then turn the ON/Oven Timer dial to 10 minutes. 6. Let the Cuisinart Air Fryer Oven work. Serve warm and enjoy.
Per Serving: Calories 282; Fat 9g; Sodium 116mg; Carbs 44.5g; Fiber 4.7g; Sugar 15.6 g; Protein 5.7 g

Banana and Walnuts Bread

Prep time: 10 minutes | Cook time: 10 minutes | Serves: 2

¼ cup flour
½ teaspoon baking powder
¼ cup mashed banana
¼ cup butter

1 tablespoon chopped walnuts
¼ cup oats
Sugar, as needed

1. Spray 4 muffin molds with cooking spray and set aside. In a bowl, mix together mashed bananas, walnuts, sugar, and butter. 2. In another bowl, mix oat flour, and baking powder. Combine the flour mixture to the banana mixture. Pour batter into prepared muffin mold. 3. Arrange the muffin mold in the Baking Pan. Insert the Baking Pan into rack Position 1. Set the Function Dial to Bake. Set Temperature Dial to 325 degrees F, and then turn the ON/Oven Timer dial to 10 minutes. Let the Cuisinart Air Fryer Oven work. 4. Carefully, invert the muffins onto the wire rack to completely cool before serving.
Per Serving: Calories 192; Fat 12.3g; Sodium 116mg; Carbs 19.4g; Fiber 4.7g; Sugar 15.6 g; Protein 1.9 g

Chili Nut Mix

Prep time: 05 minutes | Cook time: 05 minutes | Serves: 6

2 cups mix nuts
1 teaspoon ground cumin
1 teaspoon chili powder

1 tablespoon melted butter
1 teaspoon salt
1 teaspoon pepper

1. Set all ingredients in a large bowl and toss until well coated. Line the Air Fryer Basket with parchment paper and arrange the food in it. 2. Place the Air Fryer Basket onto the Baking Pan and insert into rack Position 2. Set the Function Dial to Air Fry. Set Temperature Dial to 330 degrees F, and then turn the ON/Oven Timer dial to 5 minutes. 3. Let the Cuisinart Air Fryer Oven work. Place the dish onto a wire rack to cool for about 10 minutes. 4. Serve and enjoy.
Per Serving: Calories 438; Fat 38.3g; Sodium 618mg; Carbs 18.4g; Fiber 6.6g; Sugar 0.1 g; Protein 12.9 g

Glazed Sweet Rolls

Prep time: 15 minutes | Cook time: 05 minutes | Serves: 8

1½ tablespoon cinnamon
¾ cup brown sugar
¼ cup melted coconut oil
1 to pound frozen bread dough, thawed
Glaze:

½ teaspoon vanilla
1 ¼ cup powdered erythritol
2 tablespoons softened ghee
2 ounces softened cream cheese

1. Lay out bread dough and roll out into a rectangle. Brush melted ghee over dough and leave a 1-inch border along the edges. 2. Mix cinnamon and sweetener together and then sprinkle over the dough. Roll dough tightly and slice into 8 pieces. Let sit 1 to 2 hours to rise. 3. To make the glaze, simply mix ingredients together till smooth. Place the rolls over the Baking Pan. Insert the Baking Pan into rack Position 1. 4. Set the Function Dial to Bake. Set Temperature Dial to 350 degrees F, and then turn the ON/Oven Timer dial to 5 minutes. Let the Cuisinart Air Fryer Oven work. 5. Serve rolls drizzled in cream cheese glaze. Enjoy!
Per Serving: Calories 390; Fat 8g; Sodium 268mg; Carbs 64.8g; Fiber 1.6g; Sugar 15g; Protein 5.4 g

Vanilla Puffed up

Prep time: 20 minutes | Cook time: 32 minutes | Serves: 6

¼ cup all to purpose flour
1 cup whole milk
2 teaspoons vanilla extract
1 teaspoon cream of tartar
1 vanilla bean

4 egg yolks
1-ounce sugar
¼ cup softened butter
¼ cup sugar
5 egg whites

1. Combine flour and butter in a bowl until the mixture becomes a smooth paste. Set the pan over medium flame to heat the milk. 2. Add sugar and stir until dissolved. Mix in the vanilla bean and bring to a boil. Beat the mixture using a wire whisk as you add the butter and flour mixture. 3. Lower the heat to simmer until thick. Discard the vanilla bean. Turn off the heat. Place them on an ice bath and allow to cool for 10 minutes. 4. Grease 6 ramekins with butter. Sprinkle each with a bit of sugar. Beat the egg yolks in a bowl. 5. Add the vanilla extract and milk mixture. 6. Mix until combined. Whisk together the tartar cream, egg whites, and sugar until it forms medium stiff peaks. 7. Gradually fold egg whites into the soufflé base. Transfer the mixture to the ramekins. Arrange the ramekins in the Baking Pan. 8. Insert the Baking Pan into rack Position 1. Set the Function Dial to Bake. 9. Set Temperature Dial to 330 degrees F, and then turn the ON/ Oven Timer dial to 16 minutes. Let the Cuisinart Air Fryer Oven work. 10. When cooking time is complete, remove the cups from Air Fryer and place onto a wire rack to cool for about 10 minutes. 11. Sprinkle powdered sugar on top and drizzle with chocolate sauce before serving.
Per Serving: Calories 201; Fat 12.4g; Sodium 61mg; Carbs 14.4g; Fiber 0.1g; Sugar 7.3 g; Protein 6.7 g

Filling Cheesecake

Prep time: 20 minutes | Cook time: 20 minutes | Serves: 8

Crust
½ cup dates, chopped, soaked in water for at least 15 min, soaking liquid reserved
½ cup walnuts
1 cup quick oats
Filling
½ cup vanilla almond milk
¼ cup coconut palm sugar

½ cup coconut flour
1 cup cashews, soaked in water for at least 2 hours
1 teaspoon vanilla extract
2 tablespoons lemon juice
1 to 2 teaspoon grated lemon zest
½ cup fresh berries or 6 figs, sliced
1 tablespoon arrowroot powder

1. In a food processor, process together all the crust ingredients until smooth and press the mixture into the bottom of a spring form pan. 2. Add cashews along with soaking liquid to a blender and process them until very smooth; add milk, palm sugar, coconut flour, lemon juice, lemon zest, and vanilla and blend until well combined; add arrowroot and continue blending until mixed and pour into the crust. Smooth the top. 3. Arrange the food in the Baking Pan. Insert the Baking Pan into rack Position 1. Set the Function Dial to Bake. 4. Set Temperature Dial to 375 degrees F, and then turn the ON/Oven Timer dial to 20 minutes. 5. Let the Cuisinart Air Fryer Oven work. When cooking time is complete, remove the cups and place onto a wire rack to cool for about 10 minutes. 6. Serve! Top with fruit to serve.
Per Serving: Calories 303; Fat 17.2g; Sodium 55mg; Carbs 33.7g; Fiber 3.8g; Sugar 9.2 g; Protein 7.4 g

Salty Corn

Prep time: 10 minutes | Cook time: 40 minutes | Serves: 8

2 cups giant white corn
3 tablespoons olive oil

1 to ½ teaspoons sea salt

1. Soak the corn in a bowl of water for at least 8 hours or overnight; drain and spread in a single layer on a baking tray; pat dry with paper towels. 2. In a bowl, mix corn, olive oil and salt and toss to coat well. Arrange them to the cups and place in the Baking Pan. Insert the Baking Pan into rack Position 1. 3. Set the Function Dial to Bake. Set Temperature Dial to 400 degrees F, and then turn the ON/Oven Timer dial to 20 minutes. 4. Let the Cuisinart Air Fryer Oven work. When cooking time is complete, remove the cups and place onto a wire rack to cool for about 10 minutes. 5. Serve. Let cool before serving.
Per Serving: Calories 78; Fat 5.6g; Sodium 356mg; Carbs 7.7g; Fiber 0.8g; Sugar 1.3g; Protein 1.1g

Luscious Fruit Cake

Prep time: 05 minutes | Cook time: 45 minutes | Serves: 8

Dry Ingredients
⅛ teaspoon sea salt
½ teaspoon baking powder
½ teaspoon baking soda

½ teaspoon ground cardamom
1 to ¼ cup whole wheat flour

Wet Ingredients
2 tablespoons coconut oil
½ cup unsweetened nondairy milk
2 tablespoons ground flax seeds
¼ cup agave

1 to ½ cups water
Mix to Ins
½ cup chopped cranberries
1 cup chopped pear

1. Grease the Baking Pan and set aside. In a mixing, mix all dry ingredients together. 2. In another bowl, combine together the wet ingredients; whisk the wet ingredients into the dry until smooth. 3. Fold in the add to ins and spread the mixture into the pan. Insert the Baking Pan into rack Position 1. Set the Function Dial to Bake. 4. Set Temperature Dial to 370 degrees F, and then turn the ON/Oven Timer dial to 35 minutes. Let the Cuisinart Air Fryer Oven work. 5. When cooking time is complete, remove the pan from Air Fryer and place onto a wire rack to cool for about 10 minutes 6. Serve. Let cool before serving. Enjoy!
Per Serving: Calories 309; Fat 27g; Sodium 278mg; Carbs 33.7g; Fiber 2.8g; Sugar 6.3g; Protein 4.1g

Nutty Berry Slices

Prep time: 10 minutes | Cook time: 30 minutes | Serves: 4

4 cups fresh or frozen mixed berries
1 cup almond meal
½ cup almond butter

1 cup oven roasted walnuts, sunflower seeds, pistachios.
½ teaspoon ground cinnamon

1. Crush the nuts using a mortar and pestle. In a bowl, combine the nut mix, almond meal, and cinnamon and combine well. 2. In a pie dish, spread half the nut mixture over the bottom of the Baking Pan, then top with the berries and finish with the rest of the nut mixture. 3. Insert the Baking Pan into rack Position 1. Set the Function Dial to Bake. Set Temperature Dial to 350 degrees F, and then turn the ON/Oven Timer dial to 35 minutes. 4. Let the Cuisinart Air Fryer Oven work. When cooking time is complete, remove the pan from Air Fryer and place onto a wire rack to cool for about 10 minutes. 5. Let cool before serving. Enjoy!
Per Serving: Calories 278; Fat 15.4g; Sodium 1mg; Carbs 23.7g; Fiber 8.8g; Sugar 11.3g; Protein 7.8 g

Cranberry Brownies

Prep time: 10 minutes | Cook time: 35 minutes | Serves: 10

1 to ½ cups unsweetened shredded coconut
½ cup dried cranberries
½ cup golden flax meal
½ cup coconut butter

1 cup hemp seeds
A good pinch of sea salt
Stevia, as needed

1. Combine the cranberries, flax, and hemp seeds in the bowl of your food processor and pulse until well to ground. 2. Add the shredded coconut, coconut butter, stevia, and salt and pulse until it forms thick dough. Transfer the dough to the Baking Pan. Insert the Baking Pan into rack Position 1. Set the Function Dial to Bake. 3. Set Temperature Dial to 370 degrees F, and then turn the ON/Oven Timer dial to 10 minutes. Let the Cuisinart Air Fryer Oven work. 4. When cooking time is complete, remove the pan from Air Fryer and place onto a wire rack to cool for about 10 minutes. 5. Let cool before serving. Enjoy!
Per Serving: Calories 245; Fat 21.1g; Sodium 47mg; Carbs 8.5g; Fiber 5.8g; Sugar 1.8g; Protein 6.8 g

Sweet Avocado Bars

Prep time: 05 minutes | Cook time: 25 minutes | Serves: 4

1 cup chopped chocolate
2 ripe avocados
1 teaspoon raw honey
2 teaspoons vanilla extract

4 eggs
1 cup ground almonds
½ cup cocoa powder
¼ teaspoon salt

1. Add chocolate to a bowl and place over a large saucepan of boiling water. Stir until chocolate is melted. 2. Remove from heat and let cool. In a bowl, mash the avocados; add honey and stir to combine. Whisk in vanilla extract and eggs until well blended. 3. Gradually whisk in the chocolate until well incorporated. Stir in ground almonds, cocoa powder, and salt until well blended. 4. Transfer the batter to the Baking Pan and cover with parchment paper. Insert the Baking Pan into rack Position 1. Set the Function Dial to Bake. Set Temperature Dial to 375 degrees F, and then turn the ON/Oven Timer dial to 30 minutes. 5. Let the Cuisinart Air Fryer Oven work. When cooking time is complete, remove the pan from Air Fryer and place onto a wire rack to cool for about 10 minutes. 6. Let cool before serving.
Per Serving: Calories 665; Fat 49.7g; Sodium 251mg; Carbs 46.5g; Fiber 14.3g; Sugar 25.4g; Protein 17.6 g

Nutmeg Banana Pudding

Prep time: 05 minutes | Cook time: 60 minutes | Serves: 8

1 cup caster sugar
1½ cups self to rising flour, sifted
⅓ cup butter, melted and cooled
1 teaspoon vanilla extract
¼ cup mashed banana
1 egg, lightly beaten

¾ cups milk
½ cup packed brown sugar
⅛ teaspoon nutmeg
1 teaspoon cinnamon
½ cups boiling water
Ice cream, to serve

1. Grease the Baking Pan with butter using wax paper. Combine the caster sugar, flour, butter, vanilla extract, banana, egg, and milk in a large mixing bowl. Sift sugar, nutmeg, and cinnamon over the pudding mix. 2. Spoon the boiling water gently and evenly over the mixture. Insert the Baking Pan into rack Position 1. Set the Function Dial to Bake. 3. Set Temperature Dial to 375 degrees F, and then turn the ON/Oven Timer dial to 60 minutes. Let the Cuisinart Air Fryer Oven work. 4. When cooking time is complete, remove the pan from Air Fryer and place onto a wire rack to cool for about 10 minutes. 5. Let cool before serving. Enjoy!
Per Serving: Calories 307; Fat 9g; Sodium 76mg; Carbs 54.3g; Fiber 0.9g; Sugar 25.4g; Protein 4 g

Chocolate Lava Cake

Prep time: 5 minutes | Cook time: 1 hour 10 minutes | Serves: 8

1 box of Devil's Food Chocolate Cake mix, prepared according to box instructions

1 (15 ounce) can of milk chocolate frosting, divided
Non to stick cooking spray

1. Spray the Baking Pan with cooking spray. Add cake batter prepared as instructed on the box. Spoon half of the chocolate frosting into the middle of the cake batter. 2. Insert the Baking Pan into rack Position 1. Set the Function Dial to Bake. Set Temperature Dial to 375 degrees F, and then turn the ON/Oven Timer dial to 60 minutes. 3. Let the Cuisinart Air Fryer Oven work. When cooking time is complete, remove the pan from Air Fryer and place onto a wire rack to cool for about 10 minutes. 4. Serve. Let cool before serving.
Per Serving: Calories 253; Fat 11.8g; Sodium 137mg; Carbs 37.8g; Fiber 1.1g; Sugar 32.7 g; Protein 0.5 g

Banana Loaf with Walnuts

Prep time: 05 minutes | Cook time: 60 minutes | Serves: 8

1½ cup unbleached flour
½ cup sugar or sugar substitute
2 teaspoons baking powder
½ teaspoon baking soda
½ teaspoon vanilla extract
½ teaspoon sea salt

1 cup ripe bananas, mashed
⅓ cup softened butter
¼ cup milk
1 egg
¼ cup walnuts chopped

1. Combine the flour, sugar, baking powder, baking soda and salt in a large mixing bowl; whisk until the ingredients are well mixed. 2. Fold in the bananas, butter, milk, egg and vanilla extract. Use an electric mixer to mix until the batter has a uniform thick consistency. Fold in chopped walnuts. 3. Grease the Baking Pan with non to stick cooking spray. Pour batter into it. 4. Insert the Baking Pan into rack Position 1. Set the Function Dial to Bake. Set Temperature Dial to 375 degrees F, and then turn the ON/Oven Timer dial to 60 minutes. Let the Cuisinart Air Fryer Oven work. 5. When cooking time is complete, remove the pan from Air Fryer and place onto a wire rack to cool for about 10 minutes. 6. Let cool before serving.
Per Serving: Calories 255; Fat 11g; Sodium 211mg; Carbs 36.1g; Fiber 1.4g; Sugar 32.7 g; Protein 4.6g

Choco Mug Cake

Prep time: 05 minutes | Cook time: 20 minutes | Serves: 1

1 teaspoon softened butter
1 egg
1 teaspoon butter
1 teaspoon vanilla extract

2 tablespoons Erythritol
2 tablespoons unsweetened cocoa powder
¼ teaspoon baking powder
1 tablespoon heavy cream

1. Combine all ingredients in a mixing bowl. Pour into a greased mug. 2. Arrange the mug in the Baking Pan. Insert the Baking Pan into rack Position 1. Set the Function Dial to Bake. Set Temperature Dial to 400 degrees F, and then turn the ON/Oven Timer dial to 20 minutes. 3. Let the Cuisinart Air Fryer Oven work. When cooking time is complete, remove the pan from Air Fryer and place onto a wire rack to cool for about 10 minutes. 4. Serve. Let cool before serving.
Per Serving: Calories 220; Fat 19g; Sodium 125mg; Carbs 37.7g; Fiber 3.6g; Sugar 31.1 g; Protein 8.1 g

Coconut Raspberry

Prep time: 05 minutes | Cook time: 20 minutes | Serves: 12

1 teaspoon vanilla bean
1 cup pulsed raspberries
1 cup coconut milk

3 cups desiccated coconut
¼ cup coconut oil
⅓ cup Erythritol powder

1. Combine all ingredients in a mixing bowl, and pour into the Baking Pan. Insert the Baking Pan into rack Position 1. Set the Function Dial to Bake. Set Temperature Dial to 375 degrees F, and then turn the ON/Oven Timer dial to 20 minutes. 2. Let the Cuisinart Air Fryer Oven work. When cooking time is complete, remove the pan from Air Fryer and place onto a wire rack to cool for about 10 minutes. 3. Serve. Let cool before serving.
Per Serving: Calories 152; Fat 14.2g; Sodium 9mg; Carbs 9.3g; Fiber 2.3g; Sugar 2.6 g; Protein 1.3 g

Almond Cherry Bars

Prep time: 05 minutes | Cook time: 35 minutes | Serves: 12

1 tablespoon Xanthan gum
1½ cup almond flour
½ teaspoon salt
1 cup pitted fresh cherries
½ cup softened butter

2 eggs
¼ cup water
½ teaspoon vanilla
1 cup Erythritol

1. Combine almond flour, softened butter, salt, vanilla, eggs, and erythritol in a large bowl until you form a dough. Press the dough in the Baking Pan. 2. Arrange the ramekins in the Baking Pan. Insert the Baking Pan into rack Position 1. Set the Function Dial to Bake. 3. Set Temperature Dial to 375 degrees F, and then turn the ON/Oven Timer dial to 10 minutes. Let the Cuisinart Air Fryer Oven work. 4. When cooking time is complete, remove the pan from Air Fryer. Meanwhile, mix the cherries, water, and xanthan gum in a bowl. 5. Take the dough out and pour over the cherry mixture. Bake the food again for 25 minutes more at 375 degrees F in the Cuisinart Air Fryer Oven.
Per Serving: Calories 172; Fat 15.3g; Sodium 445mg; Carbs 33.3g; Fiber 9.9g; Sugar 20.6 g; Protein 4.8 g

Aroma Doughnuts

Prep time: 05 minutes | Cook time: 06 minutes | Serves: 6

1 teaspoon baking powder
½ teaspoon salt
1 tablespoon sunflower oil
¼ cup coffee

¼ cup coconut sugar
1 cup white all to purpose flour
2 tablespoons Aquafaba

1. Combine sugar, flour, baking powder, and salt in a mixing bowl. In another bowl, combine the aquafaba, sunflower oil, and coffee. 2. Mix them to form dough. Let the dough rest inside the fridge. Place the dough in the Baking Pan. Insert the Baking Pan into rack Position 1. Set the Function Dial to Bake. 3. Set Temperature Dial to 400 degrees F, and then turn the ON/Oven Timer dial to 106 minutes. 4. Let the Cuisinart Air Fryer Oven work. Let the dish cool for a while before serving.
Per Serving: Calories 101; Fat 2.7g; Sodium 197mg; Carbs 16.9g; Fiber 0.6; Sugar 0.1 g; Protein 2.2 g

Cream Strawberry Pie

Prep time: 10 minutes | Cook time: 35 minutes | Serves: 4

¼ cup heavy whipping cream
1½ teaspoons cornstarch
1½ teaspoons white sugar
½ cup water
¼ teaspoon salt
2 teaspoons butter

1½ cups hulled strawberries
1½ teaspoons white sugar
1 tablespoon diced butter
1 tablespoon butter
½ cup all to purpose flour
¾ teaspoon baking powder

1. Lightly grease the Baking Pan with cooking spray. Add water, cornstarch, and sugar. Stir to mix well. Bake them in the Cuisinart Air Fryer Oven at 390 degrees F for 10 minutes until hot and thick. 2. Add strawberries and mix well. Dot tops with 1 tablespoon butter, and then bake them at 400 degrees F for 10 minutes. 3. In a bowl, mix well salt, baking powder, sugar, and flour. Cut in 2 teaspoons of butter. Mix in cream. 4. Spoon the mixture on the top of berries. Bake them at 390 degrees F for 15 minutes more. 5. Serve and enjoy.
Per Serving: Calories 364; Fat 5.4g; Sodium 183mg; Carbs 76.2g; Fiber 2; Sugar 18 g; Protein 2.6 g

Chocolate Caster Sugar Patty Cakes

Prep time: 05 minutes | Cook time: 12 minutes | Serves: 6

3 eggs
¼ cup caster sugar
¼ cup cocoa powder
1 teaspoon baking powder

1 cup milk
¼ teaspoon vanilla essence
2 cups all to purpose flour
4 tablespoons butter

1. Beat eggs with sugar in a bowl until creamy. Add butter and beat again for 1 to 2 minutes. 2. Now add flour, cocoa powder, milk, vanilla essence, and baking powder, mix with a spatula. Fill ¾ of muffin tins with the mixture. 3. Arrange the ramekins in the Baking Pan. Insert the Baking Pan into rack Position 1. Set the Function Dial to Bake. 4. Set Temperature Dial to 400 degrees F, and then turn the ON/Oven Timer dial to 12 minutes. Let the Cuisinart Air Fryer Oven work. 5. When cooking time is complete, remove the cups from Air Fryer and place onto a wire rack to cool for about 10 minutes. 6. Serve!
Per Serving: Calories 268; Fat 6.6g; Sodium 53mg; Carbs 44.7g; Fiber 2.2g; Sugar 10.5 g; Protein 9.1 g

Cayenne Peanuts

Prep time: 10 minutes | Cook time:20 minutes | Serves: 8

1 cup raw peanuts
½ teaspoon cayenne pepper
3 teaspoons seafood seasoning

2 tablespoons olive oil
Salt

1. In a bowl, whisk together cayenne pepper, olive oil, and seafood seasoning; stir in peanuts until well coated. Transfer the food to the Baking Pan. 2. Insert the Baking Pan into rack Position 1. Set the Function Dial to Bake. Set Temperature Dial to 380 degrees F, and then turn the ON/Oven Timer dial to 10 minutes. Let the Cuisinart Air Fryer Oven work. 3. When cooking time is complete, remove the cups from Air Fryer and place onto a wire rack to cool for about 10 minutes. 4. Top the dish with fruit to serve. Transfer the peanuts to a dish and season with salt. Let cool before serving.
Per Serving: Calories 134; Fat 12.5g; Sodium 23mg; Carbs 3g; Fiber 1.6g; Sugar 0.7 g; Protein 4.7 g

Conclusion

The Cuisinart Air Fryer Toaster Oven is a versatile appliance that can be used for a variety of cooking tasks. While it functions primarily as an air fryer, it can also be used as a toaster oven, increasing its versatility. The Air Fryer Toaster Oven also has a number of features that make it user-friendly, such as a digital display and easy-to-use controls. Overall, the Cuisinart Air Fryer Toaster Oven is a great option for everyone looking for an appliance that can do more than just one thing.

Appendix 1 Measurement Conversion Chart

VOLUME EQUIVALENTS (LIQUID)

US STANDARD	US STANDARD (OUNCES)	METRIC (APPROXIMATE)
2 tablespoons	1 fl.oz	30 mL
¼ cup	2 fl.oz	60 mL
½ cup	4 fl.oz	120 mL
1 cup	8 fl.oz	240 mL
1½ cup	12 fl.oz	355 mL
2 cups or 1 pint	16 fl.oz	475 mL
4 cups or 1 quart	32 fl.oz	1 L
1 gallon	128 fl.oz	4 L

TEMPERATURES EQUIVALENTS

FAHRENHEIT (F)	CELSIUS (C) (APPROXIMATE)
225 °F	107 °C
250 °F	120 °C
275 °F	135 °C
300 °F	150 °C
325 °F	160 °C
350 °F	180 °C
375 °F	190 °C
400 °F	205 °C
425 °F	220 °C
450 °F	235 °C
475 °F	245 °C
500 °F	260 °C

VOLUME EQUIVALENTS (DRY)

US STANDARD	METRIC (APPROXIMATE)
⅛ teaspoon	0.5 mL
¼ teaspoon	1 mL
½ teaspoon	2 mL
¾ teaspoon	4 mL
1 teaspoon	5 mL
1 tablespoon	15 mL
¼ cup	59 mL
½ cup	118 mL
¾ cup	177 mL
1 cup	235 mL
2 cups	475 mL
3 cups	700 mL
4 cups	1 L

WEIGHT EQUIVALENTS

US STANDARD	METRIC (APPROXIMATE)
1 ounce	28 g
2 ounces	57 g
5 ounces	142 g
10 ounces	284 g
15 ounces	425 g
16 ounces (1 pound)	455 g
1.5 pounds	680 g
2 pounds	907 g

Appendix 2 Air Fryer Cooking Chart

Fish and Seafood	Temp	Time (min)
Calamari (8 oz.)	400°F	4
Fish Fillet (1-inch, 8 oz.)	400°F	10
Salmon Fillet (6 oz.)	380°F	12
Tuna Steak	400°F	7 to 10
Scallops	400°F	5 to 7
Shrimp	400°F	5

Frozen Foods	Temp	Time (min)
Onion Rings (12 oz.)	400°F	8
Thin French Fries (20 oz.)	400°F	14
Thick French Fries (17 oz.)	400°F	18
Pot Sticks (10 oz.)	400°F	8
Fish Sticks (10 oz.)	400°F	10
Fish Fillets (½-inch, 10 oz.)	400°F	14

vegetables	Temp	Time (min)
Asparagus (1-inch slices)	400°F	5
Beets (sliced)	350°F	25
Beets (whole)	400°F	40
Bell Peppers (sliced)	350°F	13
Broccoli	400°F	6
Brussels Sprouts (halved)	380°F	15
Carrots(½-inch slices)	380°F	15
Cauliflower (florets)	400°F	12
Eggplant (1½-inch cubes)	400°F	15
Fennel (quartered)	370°F	15
Mushrooms (¼-inch slices)	400°F	5
Onion (pearl)	400°F	10
nips (½-inch chunks)	380°F	5
pers (1-inch chunks)	400°F	15
otatoes (baked, whole)	400°F	40
quash (½-inch chunks)	400°F	12
Tomatoes (cherry)	400°F	4
Zucchni (½-inch sticks)	400°F	12

Meat	Temp	Time (min)
Bacon	400°F	5 to 7
Beef Eye Round Roast (4 lbs.)	390°F	50 to 60
Burger (4 oz.)	370°F	16 to 20
Chicken Breasts, bone-in (1.25 lbs.)	370°F	25
Chicken Breasts, boneless (4 oz.)	380°F	12
Chicken Drumsticks (2.5 lbs.)	370°F	20
Chicken Thighs, bone-in (2 lbs.)	380°F	22
Chicken Thighs, boneless (1.5 lbs.)	380°F	18 to 20
Chicken Legs, bone-in (1.75 lbs.)	380°F	30
Chicken Wings (2 lbs.)	400°F	12
Flank Steak (1.5 lbs.)	400°F	12
Game Hen (halved, 2 lbs.)	390°F	20
Loin (2 lbs.)	360°F	55
London Broil (2 lbs.)	400°F	20 to 28
Meatballs (3-inch)	380°F	10
Rack of Lamb (1.5-2 lbs.)	380°F	22
Sausages	380°F	15
Whole Chicken (6.5 lbs.)	360°F	75

Appendix 3 Recipes Index

Printed in Great Britain
by Amazon

32773481R00063